# TEACHINGS
*of the*
# BUDDHA

# TEACHINGS

## *of the*

# BUDDHA

---

EDITED BY

*Jack Kornfield*

WITH

*Gil Fronsdal*

SHAMBHALA
*Boston & London*
2007

SHAMBHALA PUBLICATIONS, INC.
Horticultural Hall
300 Massachusetts Avenue
Boston, Massachusetts 02115
*www.shambhala.com*

9 8 7 6 5 4 3 2

PRINTED IN THE UNITED STATES OF AMERICA
Distributed in the United States by Random House, Inc.,
and in Canada by Random House of Canada Ltd

First Mass Market Edition: October 2007
ISBN 978-1-59030-508-9

*Dedicated to*
*Mahaghosananda*
*A. T. Ariyaratne*
*and*
*Tenzin Gyatso*
*who keep the lamp of the Dharma alive*

# CONTENTS

## Contents

# Contents

# Contents

# Contents

# EDITOR'S PREFACE

I T is said that soon after his enlightenment the Buddha passed a man on the road who was struck by the Buddha's extraordinary radiance and peaceful presence. The man stopped and asked, "My friend, what are you? Are you a celestial being or a god?"

"No," said the Buddha.

"Well, then, are you some kind of magician or wizard?" Again the Buddha answered, "No."

"Are you a man?"

"No."

"Well, my friend, then what are you?" The Buddha replied, "I am awake."

The word *buddha* means "one who is awake." It is the experience of awakening to the truth of life that is offered in the Buddhist tradition. For twenty-five hundred years the practices and teachings of Buddhism have offered a systematic way to see clearly and live wisely. They have offered a way to discover liberation within our own bodies and minds, in the midst of this very world.

History records that the Buddha was born as a prince in an ancient kingdom of northern India. Although as a youth he was protected by his father in beautiful palaces, as he grew older the Buddha encountered what we must all face: the inevitable sorrows of life. He saw the loss of all things we hold dear, and the aging, sickness, and death that come to every human being. Seeing this, he chose to renounce his royal title and leave his palace to become a seeker of truth, searching for the end of human sorrow, searching for freedom in the face of the ceaseless round of birth and death.

For some years the Buddha practiced as an austere yogi in the forests of India. In time he realized that his extreme asceticism had brought him no more freedom than his previous indulgence in worldly pleasure. Instead, he saw that human freedom must come from practicing a life of inner and outer balance, and he called this discovery the Middle Path.

Having seen this, the Buddha seated himself under a great banyan tree and vowed to find liberation in the face of the forces that bring suffering to humankind. He felt himself assailed by these forces—by fear, attachment, greed, hatred, delusion, temptation, and doubt. The Buddha sat in the midst of these forces with his heart open and his mind clear until he could see to the depths of human consciousness, until he discovered a place of peace at the center of them all. This was his enlightenment, the discovery of *nirvana,* the freeing of his heart from entanglement in all the conditions of the world. The realization of truth that he touched that night was so profound that his teachings about it have continued to inspire and enlighten people all over the world to this day. Over the centuries, one and a half billion people, one quarter of the human race, have followed the Buddha's way.

From the Buddha's enlightenment, two great powers were awakened in him: transcendent wisdom and universal compassion. Setting in motion the Wheel of the Dharma, the Buddha wandered first to the Deer Park in Benares and gave instructions to the yogis who had practiced with him in the forest. After this, for forty-five years he brought the teachings of wisdom and compassion to all who would listen. These teachings, which the Buddha called the Dharma, or Way, are an invitation to follow the path of enlightenment. They are an invitation to all who hear them to discover their own buddha-nature, the freedom and great heart of compassion that is possible for every human being.

To bring about the awakening of students of all temperaments, the Buddha taught a wonderful variety of spiritual practices. There are foundation practices for the development of loving-kindness, generosity, and moral integrity, the universal ground of spiritual life. Then there is a vast array of meditation practices to train the mind and open the heart. These practices include awareness of the breath and body, mindfulness of feelings and thoughts, practices of *mantra* and devotion, visualization and contemplative reflection, and practices leading to refined and profoundly expanded states of consciousness.

To carry on these teachings, the Buddha created an

ordained *sangha,* what is now one of the oldest surviving monastic orders on earth. These monks and nuns, who still number in the hundreds of thousands around the globe, follow the Buddha through a life of renunciation. But the teachings he left were not limited to renunciates. They can be understood and awakened in the heart of human beings in every circumstance, in every walk of life. The essence of these teachings is offered to you in this simple volume.

The first of the texts you will find here were originally recited and passed down orally for six hundred years before being written down. Then they were inscribed on palm leaves in ancient languages such as Pali and Sanskrit, or preserved in translations into Chinese and Tibetan. The passages in the latter portion of this book come from great Indian, Chinese, Japanese, and Tibetan *bodhisattvas,* awakened beings who follow and teach in the spirit of the Buddha. Although these later selections are not from the historical Buddha, they are included for their beauty and the authenticity with which they express the Buddha Dharma. According to Buddhist teachings, the true Buddha is not limited to the body or mind of a particular man who lived long ago. This is illustrated by the tale of a young monk who had spent weeks sitting, enraptured, at the feet of the Buddha, gazing at his form and listening to his words. Finally the Buddha chastised him, saying, "You do not even see me. To see the Buddha, you must see the Dharma, the truth. One who sees the Dharma sees me."

As you read the teachings in this book, remember that they are not meant to be philosophy, poetry, or spiritual studies for you to consider. They are words of truth that can bring you to awakening. Most of these words are so powerful that when they were first spoken, all who were present to hear them were awakened; their eyes and ears opened, and a true inner freedom was discovered.

Go through these pages little by little, savor them in your heart. Let them enter your being and resonate within you, so that you too may be awakened.

May the truth of these teachings awaken transcendent wisdom and a great heart of compassion in all beings. May they bring blessings to all.

JACK KORNFIELD
*Spirit Rock Center*
*Woodacre, California*

# TEACHINGS
*of the*
# BUDDHA

# WAKEFULNESS

WAKEFULNESS is the way to life.
The fool sleeps
As if he were already dead,
But the master is awake
And he lives forever.

He watches.
He is clear.

How happy he is!
For he sees that wakefulness is life.
How happy he is,
Following the path of the awakened.

With great perseverance
He meditates, seeking
Freedom and happiness.

*from the* DHAMMAPADA,
*translated by Thomas Byrom*

# LUMINOUS MIND

LUMINOUS is this mind, brightly shining, but it is colored by the attachments that visit it. This unlearned people do not really understand, and so do not cultivate the mind. Luminous is this mind, brightly shining, and it is free of the attachments that visit it. This the noble follower of the way really understands; so for them there is cultivation of the mind.

*from the* ANGUTTARA NIKAYA,
*translated by Gil Fronsdal*

# THE SAGE

A PERSON of wisdom should be truthful, without arrogance, without deceit, not slanderous and not hateful. The wise person should go beyond the evil of greed and miserliness.

To have your mind set on calmness, you must take power over sleepiness, drowsiness and lethargy. There is no place for laziness and no recourse to pride.

Do not be led into lying, do not be attached to forms. You must see through all pride and fare along without violence.

Do not get excited by what is old, do not be contented with what is new. Do not grieve for what is lost or be controlled by desire.

*adapted from the* SUTTA-NIPATA,
*translated by H. Saddhatissa*

# DHAMMAPADA

WE are what we think.
  All that we are arises with our thoughts.
With our thoughts we make the world.
Speak or act with an impure mind
And trouble will follow you
As the wheel follows the ox that draws the cart.

We are what we think.
All that we are arises with our thoughts.
With our thoughts we make the world.
Speak or act with a pure mind
And happiness will follow you
As your shadow, unshakable.
How can a troubled mind
Understand the way?

Your worst enemy cannot harm you
As much as your own thoughts, unguarded.

But once mastered,
No one can help you as much,
Not even your father or your mother.

*from the* DHAMMAPADA,
*translated by Thomas Byrom*

# METTA SUTTA

THIS is the work of those who are skilled and peaceful, who seek the good:

May they be able and upright, straightforward, of gentle speech and not proud.
May they be content and easily supported, unburdened, with their senses calmed.
May they be wise, not arrogant and without desire for the possessions of others.
May they do nothing mean or that the wise would reprove.

May all beings be happy.
May they live in safety and joy.
All living beings, whether weak or strong, tall, stout, average or short, seen or unseen, near or distant, born or to be born, may they all be happy.

Let no one deceive another or despise any being in any state, let none by anger or hatred wish harm to another.

As a mother watches over her child, willing to risk her own life to protect her only child, so with a boundless heart should one cherish all living

5

beings, suffusing the whole world with unobstructed loving-kindness.

Standing or walking, sitting or lying down, during
all one's waking hours, may one remain mindful
of this heart and this way of living that is the best
in the world.

Unattached to speculations, views and sense desires,
with clear vision, such a person will never be reborn in the cycles of suffering.

*version by* GIL FRONSDAL

# DEVELOPING

# LOVING-KINDNESS

PUT away all hindrances, let your mind full of love
pervade one quarter of the world, and so too the
second quarter, and so the third, and so the fourth.
And thus the whole wide world, above, below, around
and everywhere, altogether continue to pervade with
love-filled thought, abounding, sublime, beyond
measure, free from hatred and ill-will.

*adapted from the* DIGHA NIKAYA,
*translated by Maurice Walshe*

# HARMLESSNESS

ALL beings tremble before violence.
All fear death.
All love life.

See yourself in others.
Then whom can you hurt?
What harm can you do?

He who seeks happiness
By hurting those who seek happiness
Will never find happiness.

For your brother is like you.
He wants to be happy.
Never harm him
And when you leave this life
You too will find happiness.

*from the* DHAMMAPADA,
*translated by Thomas Byrom*

# VIRTUE

THE perfume of sandalwood,
  Rosebay or jasmine
Cannot travel against the wind.

But the fragrance of virtue
Travels even against the wind,
As far as the ends of the world.

Like garlands woven from a heap of flowers,
Fashion from your life as many good deeds.

*from the* DHAMMAPADA,
*translated by Thomas Byrom*

# GREAT DISCOURSE

# ON BLESSINGS

At one time the Exalted One was living in Jeta Grove. A certain deity of astounding beauty approached the Exalted One and said:

Many deities and humans
have pondered on blessings.
Tell me the blessings supreme.

The Buddha replied:

To associate not with the foolish,
to be with the wise,
to honor the worthy ones
this is a blessing supreme.

To reside in a suitable location,
to have good past deeds done,
to set oneself in the right direction
this is a blessing supreme.

To be well spoken, highly trained,
well educated, skilled in handicraft,
and highly disciplined,
this is a blessing supreme.

To be well caring of mother, of father,
to look after spouse and children,
to engage in a harmless occupation,
this is a blessing supreme.

Outstanding behavior, blameless action,
open hands to all relatives
and selfless giving,
this is a blessing supreme.

To cease and abstain from evil,
to avoid intoxicants,
to be diligent in virtuous practices,
this is a blessing supreme.

To be reverent and humble,
content and grateful,
to hear the Dharma at the right time,
this is a blessing supreme.

To be patient and obedient,
to visit with spiritual people,
to discuss the Dharma at the right time,
this is a blessing supreme.

To live austerely and purely,
to see the noble truths,
and to realize nirvana,
this is the blessing supreme.

A mind unshaken when touched
by the worldly states,
sorrowless, stainless, and secure,
this is the blessing supreme.

Those who have fulfilled all these
are everywhere invincible;
they find well-being everywhere,
theirs is the blessing supreme.

*adapted from the* MANGALA SUTTA,
*translated by Gunaratana Mahathera*

# NOBLE FRIENDSHIP

THEN the venerable Ananda approached the Lord, prostrated himself, and sat down to one side. Sitting there the venerable Ananda said to the Lord:

"Half of this holy life, Lord, is good and noble friends, companionship with the good, association with the good."

"Do not say that, Ananda. Do not say that, Ananda. It is the whole of this holy life, this friendship, companionship, and association with the good."

*from the* SAMYUTTA NIKAYA,
*translated by John Ireland*

# THE AWAKENED

How joyful to look upon the awakened
And to keep company with the wise.

Follow then the shining ones,
The wise, the awakened, the loving,
For they know how to work and forbear.

But if you cannot find
Friend or master to go with you,
Travel on alone—
Like a king who has given away his kingdom,
Like an elephant in the forest.

If the traveler can find
A virtuous and wise companion
Let him go with him joyfully
And overcome the dangers of the way.
Follow them
As the moon follows the path of the stars.

*from the* DHAMMAPADA,
*translated by Thomas Byrom*

# HATRED NEVER

# DISPELS HATE

"Look how he abused me and beat me,
How he threw me down and robbed me."
Live with such thoughts and you live in hate.

"Look how he abused me and beat me,
How he threw me down and robbed me."
Abandon such thoughts, and live in love.

In this world
Hate never yet dispelled hate.
Only love dispels hate.
This is the law,
Ancient and inexhaustible.
You too shall pass away.
Knowing this, how can you quarrel?

*from the* DHAMMAPADA,
*translated by Thomas Byrom*

# SAND CASTLES

S OME children were playing beside a river. They made castles of sand, and each child defended his castle and said, "This one is mine." They kept their castles separate and would not allow any mistakes about which was whose. When the castles were all finished, one child kicked over someone else's castle and completely destroyed it. The owner of the castle flew into a rage, pulled the other child's hair, struck him with his fist and bawled out, "He has spoiled my castle! Come along all of you and help me to punish him as he deserves." The others all came to his help. They beat the child with a stick and then stamped on him as he lay on the ground. . . . Then they went on playing in their sand castles, each saying, "This is mine; no one else may have it. Keep away! Don't touch my castle!" But evening came; it was getting dark and they all thought they ought to be going home. No one now cared what became of his castle. One child stamped on his, another pushed his over with both hands. Then they turned away and went back, each to his home.

*from the* YOGACARA BHUMI SUTRA, *translated by Arthur Waley*

# NO-SELF

THE instructed disciple of the Noble Ones does not regard material shape as self, or self as having material shape, or material shape as being in the self, or the self as being in material shape. Nor does he regard feeling, perception, the impulses, or consciousness in any of these ways. He comprehends each of these aggregates as it really is, that it is impermanent, suffering, not-self, compounded, woeful. He does not approach them, grasp after them or determine "Self for me" ["my self"]—and this for a long time conduces to his welfare and happiness.

The instructed disciple of the Noble Ones beholds of material shape, feeling, perception, the impulses, or consciousness: "This is not mine, this am I not, this is not my self." So that when the material shape, feeling, perception, the impulses, or consciousness change and become otherwise there arise not from him grief, sorrow, suffering, lamentation, and despair.

*adapted from the* SAMYUTTA NIKAYA, *translated by L. Feer*

# BODY AND MIND

WHEN body and mind dissolve, they do not exist anywhere, any more than musical notes lay heaped up anywhere. When a lute is played upon, there is no previous store of sound; and when the music ceases it does not go anywhere in space. It came into existence on account of the structure and stem of the lute and the exertions of the performer; and as it came into existence so it passes away.

In exactly the same way, all the elements of being, both corporeal and non-corporeal, come into existence after having been non-existent; and having come into existence pass away.

There is no self residing in body and mind, but the cooperation of the conformations produces what people call a person. Paradoxical though it may seem: There is a path to walk on, there is walking being done, but there is no traveler. There are deeds being done, but there is no doer. There is blowing of the air, but there is no wind that does the blowing. The thought of self is an error and all existences are as hollow as the plantain tree and as empty as twirling water bubbles.

*adapted from the* VISUDDHIMAGGA,
*translated by Henry Clarke Warren*

# DEVELOPING THE MIND

"DEVELOP a state of mind like the earth, Rahula. For on the earth people throw clean and unclean things, dung and urine, spittle, pus and blood, and the earth is not troubled or repelled or disgusted. And as you grow like the earth no contacts with pleasant or unpleasant will lay hold of your mind or stick to it.

"Similarly you should develop a state of mind like water, for people throw all manner of clean and unclean things into water and it is not troubled or repelled or disgusted. And similarly with fire, which burns all things, clean and unclean, and with air, which blows upon them all, and with space, which is nowhere established.

"Develop the state of mind of friendliness, Rahula, for, as you do so, ill-will will grow less; and of compassion, for thus vexation will grow less; and of joy, for thus aversion will grow less; and of equanimity, for thus repugnance will grow less."

*from the* MAJJHIMA NIKAYA,
*translated by A. L. Basham*

# JOY

L IVE in joy,
In love,
Even among those who hate.

Live in joy,
In health,
Even among the afflicted.

Live in joy,
In peace,
Even among the troubled.

Look within.
Be still.
Free from fear and attachment,
Know the sweet joy of the way.

*from the* DHAMMAPADA,
*translated by Thomas Byrom*

# RAIN, O SKY!

"I HAVE boiled my rice, I have milked my cows," so said the herdsman Dhaniya. "I am living together with my fellows near the banks of the Mahi river, my house is covered, the fire is kindled: therefore, if thou like, rain, O sky!"

"I am free from anger, free from stubbornness," so said the Blessed One. "I am abiding for one night near the banks of the Mahi river, my house is uncovered, the fire of craving is extinguished: therefore, if thou like, rain, O sky!"

"Gadflies are not to be found with me," so said the herdsman Dhaniya. "In meadows abounding with grass the cows are roaming, and they can endure rain when it comes: therefore, if thou like, rain, O sky!"

"By me is made a well-constructed raft," so said the Buddha. "I have passed over to Nirvana, I have reached the further bank, having overcome the torrent; there is no further use for a raft: therefore, if thou like, rain, O sky!"

"My wife is obedient, not wanton," so said the herdsman Dhaniya. "For a long time she has been living together with me, she is winning, and I hear nothing wicked of her: therefore, if thou like, rain, O sky!"

"My mind is obedient, delivered from all worldliness," so said the Buddha. "It has for a long time been highly cultivated and well-subdued, there is no longer anything wicked in me: therefore, if thou like, rain, O sky!"

"I support myself by my own earning," so said the herdsman Dhaniya. "And my children are all about me, healthy; I hear nothing wicked of them: therefore, if thou like, rain, O sky!"

"I am no one's servant," so said the Buddha. "With what I have gained I wander freely in all the world, without being subservient to anyone: therefore, if thou like, rain, O sky!"

*adapted from the* SUTTA-NIPATA,
*translated by V. Fausböll*

# HOUSE BUILDER

Before my enlightenment, while I was still only an unenlightened Bodhisattva, I thought: In the case of material form, of feeling [of pleasure, pain, or neither], of perception, of formations, of consciousness, what is the gratification, what is the danger, what is the escape? Then I thought: In the case of each the bodily pleasure and mental joy that arise in dependence on these five aggregates are the gratification; the fact that these things are all impermanent, painful, and subject to change is the danger; the disciplining and abandoning of desire and lust for them is the escape.

"As long as I did not know by direct knowledge, as it actually is, that such was the gratification, such the danger, and such the escape, in the case of these five aggregates affected by clinging, so long did I make no claim to have discovered the enlightenment that is supreme in the world with its deities, its Maras and its divinities, in this generation with its monks and brahmans, with its princes and men. But as soon as I knew by direct knowledge, as it actually is, that such is the gratification, such the danger, and such the escape, in the case of these five aggregates affected by clinging, then I claimed to have discovered the enlightenment that is supreme in the world with its deities, its Maras and its divinities, in this generation with its monks and brahmans, with its princes and men."

"Being myself subject to birth, aging, ailment, death, sorrow, and defilement, seeing danger in what is subject to those things and seeking the unborn, unaging, unailing, deathless, sorrowless, undefiled supreme surcease of bondage, nirvana, I attained it. The knowledge and vision was in me: My deliverance is unassailable; this is my last birth; there is now no renewal of being."

> "Seeking but not finding the House Builder,
> I traveled through the round of countless births:
> O painful is birth ever and again.
>> House Builder, you have now been seen;
>> You shall not build the house again.
>> Your rafters have been broken down;
>> Your ridge pole is shattered.
> My mind has attained the peace of nirvana
> And reached the end of every kind of craving."

*adapted from the* SAMYUTTA NIKAYA, MAJJHIMA NIKAYA, *and* DHAMMAPADA, *translated by Nyanamoli Thera*

# PARABLE OF THE ARROW

A MAN approached the Blessed One and wanted to have all his philosophical questions answered before he would practice.

In response, the Buddha said, "It is as if a man had been wounded by a poisoned arrow and when attended to by a physician were to say, 'I will not allow you to remove this arrow until I have learned the caste, the age, the occupation, the birthplace, and the motivation of the person who wounded me.' That man would die before having learned all this. In exactly the same way, anyone who should say, 'I will not follow the teaching of the Blessed One until the Blessed One has explained all the multiform truths of the world'—that person would die before the Buddha had explained all this."

*adapted from the* MAJJHIMA NIKAYA,
*translated by E. A. Burtt*

# DHARMA AS MEDICINE

"JUST as a capable physician might instantly cure a patient who is in pain and seriously ill; so also, dear sir, whatever one hears of the Buddha's Dharma, be it discourses, mixed prose, explanations or marvelous statements—one's sorrow, lamentation, pain, grief and despair will vanish.

"Just as if there were a beautiful pond with a pleasant shore, its water being clear, agreeable, cool and transparent, and a man came by, scorched and exhausted by the heat, fatigued, parched and thirsty, and he would step into the pond, bathe and drink, and thus all his plight, fatigue and feverishness are allayed; so also, dear sir, whenever one hears the Buddha's Dharma, be it discourses, mixed prose, explanations or marvelous statements—all one's plight, fatigue and the feverish burning of the heart are allayed."

*from the* ANGUTTARA NIKAYA,
*translated by Nyanaponika Thera*

# THE FOUR

# NOBLE TRUTHS

THE Buddha said,

"And I discovered that profound truth, so difficult to perceive, difficult to understand, tranquillizing and sublime, which is not to be gained by mere reasoning, and is visible only to the wise.

"The world, however, is given to pleasure, delighted with pleasure, enchanted with pleasure. Truly, such beings will hardly understand the law of conditionality, the dependent origination of everything. Yet there are beings whose eyes are only a little covered with dust: they will understand the truth."

What now is the Noble Truth of Suffering?

Birth is suffering; decay is suffering; death is suffering; sorrow, lamentation, pain, grief, and despair are suffering; not to get what one desires is suffering; in short the five groups of existence are suffering.

What, now, is the Noble Truth of the Origin of Suffering?

It is craving, which gives rise to fresh rebirth, and, bound up with pleasure and lust, now here, now there, finds ever-fresh delight. But where does this craving arise and take root? Wherever in the world there are delightful and pleasurable things, there this craving rises and takes root. Eye, ear, nose, tongue, body, and mind are delightful and pleasurable: there this craving arises and takes root.

Visual objects, sounds, smells, tastes, bodily impressions, and mind objects are delightful and pleasurable: there this craving arises and takes root.

Consciousness, sense impression, feeling born of sense impression, perception, will, craving, thinking, and reflection are delightful and pleasurable: there this craving arises and takes root.

What, now, is the Noble Truth of the Extinction of Suffering?

It is the complete fading away and extinction of this craving, its forsaking and abandonment, liberation and detachment from it. The extinction of greed, the extinction of hate, the extinction of delusion: this, indeed, is called Nirvana.

And for a disciple thus freed, in whose heart dwells peace, there is nothing to be added to what has been done, and naught more remains to do. Just as a rock of one solid mass remains unshaken by the wind, even so neither forms, nor sounds, nor odors, nor tastes, nor contacts of any kind, neither the desired nor the undesired can cause such a one to waver; one is steadfast in mind, gained is deliverance.

And one who has considered all the contrasts of this earth, and is no more disturbed by anything whatever in the world, the Peaceful One, freed from rage, from sorrow, and from longing, has passed beyond birth and decay.

This I call neither arising, nor passing away, neither standing still, nor being born, nor dying. There is neither foothold, nor development, nor any basis. This is the end of suffering.

Hence, the purpose of the Holy Life does not consist in acquiring alms, honor, or fame, nor in gaining morality, concentration, or the eye of knowledge. That unshakable deliverance of the heart: that, indeed, is the object of the Holy Life, that is its essence, that is its goal.

What, now, is the Noble Truth of the Path that leads to the extinction of suffering?

To give oneself up to indulgence in sensual pleasure, the base, common, vulgar, unholy, unprofitable; or to give oneself up to self-mortification, the painful, unholy, unprofitable: both these two extremes, the Perfect One has avoided, and has discovered the Middle Path, which makes one both see and know, which leads to peace, to discernment, to Nirvana.

It is the Noble Eightfold Path, the way that leads to the extinction of suffering, namely:

1. Right Understanding
2. Right Thought
3. Right Speech
4. Right Action
5. Right Livelihood
6. Right Effort

7. Right Mindfulness
8. Right Concentration

This is the Middle Path which the Perfect One has discovered, which makes one both see and know, which leads to peace, to discernment, to enlightenment.

*adapted from the* SAMYUTTA NIKAYA, *translated by Nyanatiloka*

# SICKNESS, OLD AGE,

# AND DEATH

DID you never see in the world a man, or a woman, eighty, ninety, or a hundred years old, frail, crooked as a gable-roof, bent down, resting on crutches, with tottering steps, infirm, youth long since fled, with broken teeth, gray and scanty hair or none, wrinkled, with blotched limbs? And did the thought never come to you that you also are subject to decay, that you also cannot escape it?

Did you never see in the world a man, or a woman who, being sick, afflicted, and grievously ill, wallowing in his own filth, was lifted up by some and put to bed by others? And did the thought never come to you that you also are subject to disease, that you also cannot escape it?

Did you never see in the world the corpse of a man, or a woman, one or two or three days after death, swollen up, blue-black in color, and full of corruption? And did the thought never come to you that you also are subject to death, that you also cannot escape it?

Suppose a man who was not blind beheld the many bubbles on the Ganges as they drove along, and he watched them and carefully examined them, then after he had carefully examined them they would appear to him empty, unreal and unsubstantial. In exactly the same way does the monk behold all physical phenomena, feelings, perceptions, mental formations, and states of consciousness—whether they be of the past, or the present, or the future, far or near. And he observes them, and examines them carefully; and, after carefully examining them, they appear to him empty, void, and without a Self.

*adapted from the* MAJJHIMA NIKAYA,
*translated by Nyanatiloka*

# CROSSING THE STREAM

F EW cross over the river.
Most are stranded on this side.
On the riverbank they run up and down.

But the wise person, following the way,
Crosses over, beyond the reach of death.

Free from desire,
Free from possessions,
Free from attachment and appetite,
Following the seven lights of awakening,
And rejoicing greatly in one's freedom,
In this world the wise person
Becomes oneself a light,
Pure, shining, free.

*adapted from the* DHAMMAPADA,
*translated by Thomas Byrom*

# PARABLE OF

# THE MUSTARD SEED

Gotami was her family name, but because she tired easily, she was called Kisa Gotami, or Frail Gotami. She was reborn at Savatthi in a poverty-stricken house. When she grew up, she married, going to the house of her husband's family to live. There, because she was the daughter of a poverty-stricken house, they treated her with contempt. After a time she gave birth to a son. Then they accorded her respect.

But when that boy of hers was old enough to play and run hither and about, he died. Sorrow sprang up within her. Thought she: Since the birth of my son, I, who was once denied honor and respect in this very house, have received respect. These folk may even seek to cast my son away. Taking her son on her hip, she went about from one house door to another, saying: "Give me medicine for my son!"

Wherever people encountered her, they said: "Where did you ever meet with medicine for the dead?" So saying, they clapped their hands and laughed in derision. She had not the slightest idea what they meant.

Now a certain wise man saw her and thought: This woman must have been driven out of her mind by sorrow for her son. But medicine for her, no one else is likely to know—the Sage of the Ten Forces alone is likely to know. Said he: "Woman, as for medicine for your son—there is no one else who knows—the Sage of the Ten Forces, the foremost individual in the world of men and the worlds of the gods, resides at a neighboring monastery. Go to him and ask."

The man speaks the truth, thought she. Taking her son on her hip, she took her stand in the outer circle of the congregation around the seated Buddha and said: "O Exalted One, give me medicine for my son!"

The Teacher, seeing that she was ripe for understanding, said: "You did well, Gotami, in coming hither for medicine. Go enter the city, make the rounds of the entire city, beginning at the beginning, and in whatever house no one has ever died, from that house fetch tiny grains of mustard seed."

"Very well, reverend sir," said she. Delighted in heart, she entered within the city, and at the very first house said: "The Sage of the Ten Forces bids me fetch tiny grains of mustard seed for medicine for my son. Give me tiny grains of mustard seed."

"Alas! Gotami," said they, and brought and gave to her.

"This particular seed I cannot take. In this house someone has died!"

"What say you, Gotami! Here it is impossible to count the dead!"

"Well then, enough! I'll not take it. The Sage of the Ten Forces did not tell me to take mustard seed from a house where anyone has ever died."

In this same way she went to the second house, and to the third and fourth. Finally she understood: In the entire city this must be the way! The Buddha, full of compassion for the welfare of mankind, must have seen! Overcome with emotion, she went outside of the city, carried her son to the burning-ground, and holding him in her arms, said: "Dear little son, I thought that you alone had been overtaken by this thing which men call death. But you are not the only one death has overtaken. This is a law common to all mankind." So saying, she cast her son away in the burning-ground. Then she uttered the following stanza:

No village law, no law of market town,
No law of a single house is this—
Of all the world and all the worlds of gods
This only is the Law, that all things are
    impermanent.

*from* BUDDHIST PARABLES,
*translated by E. W. Burlingame*

# THREE

# CHARACTERISTICS

"ALL formations are transient; all formations are subject to suffering; all things are without a self.

"Therefore, whatever there be of form, of feeling, perception, mental formations, or consciousness, whether past, present, or future, one's own or external, gross or subtle, lofty or low, far or near, one should understand according to reality and true wisdom: 'This does not belong to me; this am I not; this is not my Self.'"

*adapted from the*
ANGUTTARA NIKAYA *and* SAMYUTTA NIKAYA,
*translated by Nyanatiloka*

# END OF CLINGING

"JUST so, Ananda, in one who contemplates the enjoyment of all things that make for clinging, craving arises; through craving, clinging is conditioned; through clinging, the process of becoming is conditioned; through the process of becoming, rebirth is conditioned; through rebirth are conditioned old age and death, sorrow, lamentation, pain, grief, and despair. Thus arises the whole mass of suffering again in the future.

"But in the person, Ananda, who dwells contemplating the sorrow of all things that make for clinging, craving ceases; when craving ceases, clinging ceases; when clinging ceases, the process of becoming ceases; when the process of becoming ceases, rebirth ceases; when rebirth ceases, old age and death, sorrow, lamentation, pain, grief, and despair cease. Thus the entire mass of suffering ceases.

"Suppose, Ananda, there were a great tree and a man were to come with an axe and basket and were to cut down that tree at the root. After cutting it at the root he were to dig a trench and were to pull out the roots even to the rootlets and fibers of them. Then he were to cut the tree into logs and were then to split the logs and were then to make the logs into chips. Then he were to dry the chips in wind and sun, then burn them with fire, collect them into a heap of ash, then winnow the ashes in a strong wind or let them be carried away by the swift stream of a river.

"Surely that great tree thus cut down at the roots would be made as a palmtree stump, become unproductive, become unable to sprout again in the future.

"Just so, Ananda, in him who dwells contemplating the sorrow of all things that make for clinging . . . the entire mass of suffering ceases."

*from the* SAMYUTTA NIKAYA,
*translated by David Maurice*

# SUTRA ON TOTALITY

M ONKS, I will teach you the totality of life. Listen, attend carefully to it and I will speak.

What, monks, is totality? It is just the eye with the objects of sight, the ear with the objects of hearing, the nose with the objects of smell, the body with the objects of touch, and the mind with the objects of cognition. This, monks, is called totality.

Now, if anyone were to say: "Aside from this explanation of totality, I will preach another totality," that person would be speaking empty words, and being questioned would not be able to answer. Why is this? Because that person is talking about something outside of possible knowledge.

*from the* SAMYUTTA NIKAYA,
*translated by Gil Fronsdal*

# FIRE SERMON

Aɴᴅ the Blessed One went forth to Gayasisa, near Gaya, together with a company of one thousand monks.

There the Blessed One thus addressed the monks: "Everything, O monks, is burning. And how, O monks, is everything burning?

"The eye, O monks, is burning; visible things are burning; the mental impressions based on the eye are burning; the contact of the eye with visible things is burning; the sensation produced by the contact of the eye with visible things, be it pleasant, be it painful, be it neither pleasant nor painful, that also is burning. With what fire is it burning? I declare unto you that it is burning with the fire of greed, with the fire of anger, with the fire of ignorance; it is burning with the anxieties of birth, decay, death, grief, lamentation, suffering, dejection, and despair.

"The ear is burning, sounds are burning, . . . The nose is burning, odors are burning, . . . The tongue is burning, tastes are burning, . . . The body is burning, objects of contact are burning, . . . The mind is burning, thoughts are burning, all are burning with the fire of greed, of anger, and of ignorance.

"Considering this, O monks, a disciple walking in the Noble Path, becomes weary of the eye, weary of visible things, weary of the mental impressions based on the eye, weary of the contact of the eye with visible things, weary also of the sensation produced by the contact of the eye with visible things, be it pleasant, be it painful, be it neither pleasant nor painful. He or she becomes weary of the ear, and so forth ... down to ... thoughts. Becoming weary of all that, one divests oneself of grasping; by absence of grasping one is made free; when one is free, one becomes aware that one is free; and one realizes that rebirth is exhausted; and that there is no further return to this world."

When this exposition was propounded, the minds of those thousand monks became free from attachment to the world, and were released from all entanglement.

*adapted from the* MAHAVAGGA,
*translated by T. W. Rhys-Davids and Herman Oldenberg*

# MASTER YOUR SENSES

MASTER your senses,
What you taste and smell,
What you see, what you hear.

In all things be a master
Of what you do and say and think.
Be free.

Are you quiet?
Quieten your body.
Quieten your mind.

By your own efforts
Waken yourself, watch yourself,
And live joyfully.

Follow the truth of the way.
Reflect upon it.
Make it your own.
Live it.
It will always sustain you.

*from the* DHAMMAPADA,
*translated by Thomas Byrom*

# NIRVANA

NAGASENA said:
"Nirvana shares one quality with the lotus, two with water, three with medicine, ten with space, three with the wishing jewel, and five with a mountain peak. As the lotus is unstained by water, so is Nirvana unstained by all the defilements. As cool water allays feverish heat, so also Nirvana is cool and allays the fever of all the passions. Moreover, as water removes the thirst of humans and animals who are exhausted, parched, thirsty, and overpowered by heat, so also Nirvana removes the craving for sensuous enjoyments, the craving for further becoming, the craving for the cessation of becoming. As medicine protects from the torments of poison, so Nirvana from the torments of the poisonous passions. Moreover, as medicine puts an end to sickness, so Nirvana to all sufferings. Finally, Nirvana and medicine both give security. And these are the ten qualities which Nirvana shares with space. Neither is born, grows old, dies, passes away, or is reborn; both are unconquerable, cannot be stolen, are unsupported, are roads respectively for birds and Awakened Ones to journey on, are unobstructed and infinite. Like the wishing jewel, Nirvana grants all one

can desire, brings joy, and sheds light. As a mountain peak is lofty and exalted, so is Nirvana. As a mountain peak is unshakable, so is Nirvana. As a mountain peak is inaccessible, so is Nirvana inaccessible to all the passions. As no seeds can grow on a mountain peak, so the seeds of all the passions cannot grow in Nirvana. And finally, as a mountain peak is free from all desire to please or displease, so is Nirvana."

*from the* MILINDAPANHA, *translated by Edward Conze*

# MASTER YOURSELF

Love yourself and be awake—
Today, tomorrow, always.

First establish yourself in the way,
Then teach others,
And so defeat sorrow.

To straighten the crooked
You must first do a harder thing—
Straighten yourself.

You are your only master.
Who else?
Subdue yourself,
And discover your master.

*adapted from the* DHAMMAPADA,
*translated by Thomas Byrom*

# THE REFINEMENT

# OF MIND

HERE is a simile for the refinement of the mind:
There are, my friends, gross impurities in
gold, such as earth, and sand, gravel, and grit. Now the
skilled goldsmith first pours the gold into a trough and
washes, rinses, and cleans it thoroughly.

When the goldsmith has done this, there still
remain moderate impurities in the gold, such as fine
grit and coarse sand. Then the goldsmith rinses and
cleans it again.

When the goldsmith has done this, there still
remain minute impurities in the gold, such as fine
sand and dust. Now the goldsmith repeats the washing
and thereafter only the gold dust remains.

The goldsmith now pours the gold into the melting
pot and smelts it, melts it together. But the goldsmith
does not yet take it out from the vessel as the dross has
not yet been entirely removed and the gold is not yet
quite pliant, workable, and bright; it is still brittle and
does not yet lend itself to molding.

But a time comes when the goldsmith repeats the
melting so that the flaws are entirely removed. The

gold is now quite pliant, workable, and bright; and it lends itself easily to molding. Whatever ornament the goldsmith now wishes to make of it, be it a crown, earrings, a necklace, or a golden chain, the gold can now be used for that purpose.

Similarly, in the case of a practitioner devoted to practice, there may be such gross impurities as unskillful conduct in deeds, words, and thoughts. Such conduct the follower of the way gives up, puts away, lets go, and relinquishes.

When one has abandoned these there may still remain such impurities of a moderate degree as lustful, angry, and violent thoughts. Such thoughts the follower of the way gives up, puts away, lets go, and relinquishes.

When one has abandoned these, there may still remain such subtle impurities as clinging to relatives, to nation, or to one's reputation.

When one has abandoned these, there may still remain grasping to special states of meditation.

Thus concentration is not yet properly calm or refined; it has not attained to full tranquillity, nor has it achieved mental unification. But there comes a time when the practitioner's mind gains firmness within, settles down, becomes unified and concentrated. With such a concentration the practitioner is able to direct the mind to states of higher insight.

Having completed this initial purification, a follower of the way devoted to practice should from time to time direct attention to three qualities of mind. The practitioner should from time to time pay attention to the state of concentration, the state of energetic effort, and the state of equanimity.

If one gives direct attention exclusively to concentration, one's mind may fall into indolence. If one directs attention exclusively to energetic effort, one's mind may fall into restlessness. If one directs exclusive attention to equanimity, one's mind will not be well concentrated on overcoming fetters and attachments.

But if, from time to time, the practitioner pays attention to each of these qualities, the practitioner's mind will be pliant, workable, and lucid.

Suppose a goldsmith builds a furnace, lights a fire in its opening, takes the gold with a pair of tongs, and puts it into the furnace. From time to time the goldsmith blows on it, from time to time the goldsmith sprinkles water on it, from time to time the goldsmith examines it closely. If the goldsmith were to blow on the gold continuously, it might be heated too much. If the goldsmith continuously sprinkled water on it, it would be cooled. If the goldsmith were only to examine it closely, the gold would not come to perfect refinement. But if, from time to time, the goldsmith attends to each of these three functions, the gold will become pliant, workable, and bright—and it can easily be molded. Whatever ornament the goldsmith wishes to make of it, be it a crown, an earring, a necklace, or a golden chain, the gold can now be used for that purpose.

Similarly there are those three qualities to which a devoted practitioner should, from time to time, pay attention to, namely, concentration, energetic effort, and equanimity. If one gives regular attention to these, then one's mind will become pliant, workable, lucid, and not unwieldy, and it will be well concentrated upon overcoming all fetters and attachments.

*adapted from the* ANGUTTARA NIKAYA,
*translated by Nyanaponika Thera*

# PLOWING

EARLY one morning, while on his alms round, the Buddha approached the area being plowed in springtime when Bharadvaja, the Brahmin, was distributing food to his workers. When Bharadvaja saw the Buddha coming for alms he said, "I, O monk, plow and sow, and having plowed and sown, then I eat. Do you likewise plow and sow and, having plowed and sown, eat?"

The Buddha replied, "I, also, Brahmin, plow and sow and, having plowed and sown, eat."

Then Bharadvaja said, "You claim yourself to be a plowman? I see no plow! Tell me, O plowman, what kind of plowing is it you do?"

The Buddha replied, "Trust is the seed and composure the rain. Clarity is my plow and yoke, conscience is my guide-pole, and my mind is the harness. Wakefulness is my plow-blade and my goad. Well-guarded in action and in speech, and moderate in food, I use truth to weed and cultivate release. True effort is my oxen, drawing the plow steadily toward Nirvana, freedom without regret. This is how I plow, it bears the deathless as its fruit. Whoever plows in this way, will become free of all sorrow and distress."

Then Bharadvaja exclaimed, "Let the Venerable monk eat! You are indeed a plowman and your plowing bears the fruit of freedom."

*adapted from the* SAMYUTTA NIKAYA,
*translated by Gil Fronsdal*

# SERENITY AND JOY

D RINK deeply.
Live in serenity and joy.
The wise person delights in the truth
And follows the law of the awakened.

The farmer channels water to his land
The fletcher whittles his arrows.
And the carpenter turns his wood.
So the wise direct their mind.

*adapted from the* DHAMMAPADA,
*translated by Thomas Byrom*

# PATH OF MINDFULNESS

"**O**MONKS," said the Buddha, "there is a most wonderful way to help living beings realize purification, overcome directly grief and sorrow, end pain and anxiety, travel the right path, and realize Nirvana. This way is the Four Establishments of Mindfulness.

"What are the Four Establishments?

"Monks, a practitioner remains established in the observation of the body in the body, diligent, with clear understanding, mindful, having abandoned every craving and every distaste for this life.

"One remains established in the observation of the feelings in the feelings, diligent, with clear understanding, mindful, having abandoned craving and every distaste for this life.

"One remains established in the observation of the mind in the mind, diligent, with clear understanding, mindful, having abandoned every craving and every distaste for this life.

"One remains established in the observation of the objects of mind in the objects of mind, diligent, with clear understanding, mindful, having abandoned every craving and every distaste for this life."

\* \* \*

"And how does a practitioner remain established in the observation of the body in the body?

"One goes to the forest, to the foot of a tree, or to an empty room, sits down cross-legged in the lotus position, holds one's body straight, and establishes mindfulness in front of oneself. "Breathing in, one is aware of breathing in. Breathing out, one is aware of breathing out. Breathing in a long breath, one knows, 'I am breathing in a long breath.' Breathing out a long breath, one knows, 'I am breathing out a long breath.' Breathing in a short breath, one knows, 'I am breathing in a short breath.' Breathing out a short breath, one knows, 'I am breathing out a short breath.'

"Moreover, when walking, the practitioner is aware, 'I am walking'; when standing is aware, 'I am standing'; when sitting, is aware, 'I am sitting'; when lying down, is aware, 'I am lying down.' In whatever position one's body happens to be, one is aware of the position of the body.

"When one is going forward or backward, one applies full awareness to one's going forward or backward. When one looks in front or looks behind, bends down or stands up, one also applies full awareness to what one is doing. One applies full awareness to wearing the robe or carrying the alms bowl. When one eats or drinks, chews or savors the food, one applies full awareness to all this. When passing excrement or urinating, one applies full awareness to this. When one walks, stands, lies down, sits, sleeps or wakes up, speaks or is silent, one shines his awareness on all this."

* * *

"Monks, how does a practitioner remain established in the observation of the feelings in the feelings?

"Whenever the practitioner has a pleasant feeling, one is aware, 'I am experiencing a pleasant feeling.' Whenever one has a painful feeling, one is aware, 'I am experiencing a painful feeling.' Whenever one experiences a feeling which is neither pleasant nor painful, one is aware, 'I am experiencing a neutral feeling.' When one experiences a feeling based in the body, one is aware, 'I am experiencing a feeling based in the body.' When one experiences a feeling based in the mind, one is aware, 'I am experiencing a feeling based in the mind.'"

"Monks, how does a practitioner remain established in the observation of the mind in the mind?

"When one's mind is desiring, the practitioner is aware, 'My mind is desiring.' When one's mind is not desiring, one is aware, 'My mind is not desiring.' When one's mind is hating something, one is aware, 'My mind is hating.' When one's mind is not hating, one is aware, 'My mind is not hating.' When one's mind is in a state of ignorance, one is aware, 'My mind is in a state of ignorance.' When one's mind is not in a state of ignorance, one is aware, 'My mind is not in a state of ignorance.' When one's mind is tense, one is aware, 'My mind is tense.' When one's mind is not tense, one is aware, 'My mind is not tense.' When one's mind is distracted, one is aware, 'My mind is distracted.' When one's mind is not distracted, one is aware, 'My mind is not distracted.' When one's mind has a wider scope, one is aware, 'My mind has widened in scope.' When one's mind has a narrow scope, one is aware, 'My mind has become narrow in scope.'

"When one's mind is composed, one is aware, 'My mind is composed.' When one's mind is not composed, one is aware, 'My mind is not composed.' When one's mind is free, one is aware, 'My mind is free.' When one's mind is not free, one is aware, 'My mind is not free.'"

"Monks, how does a practitioner remain established in the observation of the objects of mind in the objects of mind?

"First of all, one observes the objects of mind in the objects of mind with regard to the Five Hindrances. How does one observe this?

1. "When sensual desire is present in oneself, one is aware, 'Sensual desire is present in me.' Or when sensual desire is not present in oneself, one is aware, 'Sensual desire is not present in me.' When sensual desire begins to arise, one is aware of it. When already arisen sensual desire is abandoned, one is aware of it. When sensual desire already abandoned will not arise again in the future, one is aware of it.

2. "When anger is present in oneself, one is aware, 'Anger is present in me.' When anger is not present in oneself, one is aware, 'Anger is not present in me.' When anger begins to arise, one is aware of it. When

already arisen anger is abandoned, one is aware of it. When anger already abandoned will not arise again in the future, one is aware of it.

3. "When dullness and drowsiness are present in oneself, one is aware, 'Dullness and drowsiness are present in me.' When dullness and drowsiness are not present in oneself, one is aware, 'Dullness and drowsiness are not present in me.' When dullness and drowsiness begin to arise, one is aware of it. When already arisen dullness and drowsiness are abandoned, one is aware of it. When dullness and drowsiness already abandoned will not arise again in the future, one is aware of it.

4. "When agitation and remorse are present in oneself, one is aware, 'Agitation and remorse are present in me.' When agitation and remorse are not present in oneself, one is aware, 'Agitation and remorse are not present in me.' When agitation and remorse begin to arise, one is aware of it. When already arisen agitation and remorse are abandoned, one is aware of it. When agitation and remorse already abandoned will not arise again in the future, one is aware of it.

5. "When doubt is present in oneself, one is aware, 'Doubt is present in me.' When doubt is not present in oneself, one is aware, 'Doubt is not present in me.' When doubt begins to arise, one is aware of it. When already arisen doubt is abandoned, one is aware of it. When doubt already abandoned will not arise again in the future, one is aware of it.

"This is how the practitioner remains established in

the observation of the objects of mind in the objects of mind: observation of the objects of mind from inside the objects of mind or outside the objects of mind, or observation of the objects of mind from both the inside and the outside. One remains established in the observation of the process of coming-to-be in the objects of mind or the process of dissolution in the objects of mind or both in the process of coming-to-be and the process of dissolution. Or one is mindful of the fact, 'There is an object of the mind here,' until understanding and full awareness come about. One remains established in the observation, free, not caught up in any worldly consideration. That is how to practice observation of the objects of mind in the objects of mind with regard to the Five Hindrances, O monks.

"Further, monks, the practitioner remains established in the observation of the objects of mind in the objects of mind with regard to the Seven Factors of Awakening.

"How does one remain established in the practice of observation of the Seven Factors of Awakening?

1. "When the factor of awakening, mindfulness, is present in oneself, one is aware, 'Mindfulness is present in me.' When mindfulness is not present in oneself, one is aware, 'Mindfulness is not present in me.' One is aware when not-yet-born mindfulness is being born and when already-born mindfulness is perfectly developed.

2. "When the factor of awakening, investigation-of-phenomena, is present in oneself, one is aware, 'Investigation-of-phenomena is present in me.' When investigation-of-phenomena is not present in oneself, one is aware, 'Investigation-of-phenomena is not present in me.' One is aware when not-yet-born investigation-of-phenomena is being born and when already-born investigation-of-phenomena is perfectly developed.

3. "When the factor of awakening, energy, is present in oneself, one is aware, 'Energy is present in me.' When energy is not present in oneself, one is aware, 'Energy is not present in me.' One is aware when not-yet-born energy is being born and when already-born energy is perfectly developed.

4. "When the factor of awakening, joy, is present in oneself, one is aware, 'Joy is present in me.' When joy is not present in oneself, one is aware, 'Joy is not present in me.' One is aware when not-yet-born joy is being born and when already-born joy is perfectly developed.

5. "When the factor of awakening, ease, is present in oneself, one is aware, 'Ease is present in me.' When ease is not present in oneself, one is aware, 'Ease is not present in me.' One is aware when not-yet-born ease is being born and when already-born ease is perfectly developed.

6. "When the factor of awakening, concentration, is present in oneself, one is aware, 'Concentration is present in me.' When concentration is not present in oneself, one is aware, 'Concentration is not present in me.'

One is aware when not-yet-born concentration is being born and when already-born concentration is perfectly developed.

7. "When the factor of awakening, letting go, is present in oneself, one is aware, 'Letting go is present in me.' When letting go is not present in oneself, one is aware, 'Letting go is not present in me.' One is aware when not-yet-born letting go is being born and when already-born letting-go is perfectly developed.

"This is how the practitioner remains established in the observation of the objects of mind in the objects of mind with regard to the Seven Factors of Awakening, observation of the objects of mind from inside the objects of mind or outside the objects of mind, or observation of the objects of mind from both the inside and the outside. One remains established in the observation of the process of coming-to-be in the object of mind or the process of dissolution in the object of mind or both in the process of coming-to-be and the process of dissolution. Or one is mindful of the fact, 'There is an object of mind here,' until understanding and full awareness come about. One remains established in the observation, free, not caught up in any worldly consideration. That is how to practice observation of the objects of mind in the objects of mind with regard to the Seven Factors of Awakening, O monks.

"How, monks, does the practitioner remain established in the observation of the Four Noble Truths?

"A practitioner is aware, 'This is suffering,' as it arises. One is aware, 'This is the cause of the suffering,' as it arises. One is aware, 'This is the end of suffering,' as it arises. One is aware, 'This is the path which leads to the end of suffering,' as it arises."

"Monks, one who practices in the Four Establishments of Mindfulness for seven years can expect one of two fruits—the highest understanding in this very life or, if there remains some residue of affliction, he can attain the fruit of no-return.

"Let alone seven years, monks, whoever practices in the Four Establishments of Mindfulness for six, five, four, three, two years, one year, or one month, can also expect one of two fruits—either the highest understanding in this very life or can attain the fruit of no-return.

"Let alone a month, monks, whoever practices the Four Establishments of Mindfulness one week can also expect one of two fruits—either the highest understanding in this very life or the fruit of no-return."

The monks were delighted to hear the teaching of the Buddha. They took it to heart and began to put it into practice.

*adapted from the* SATIPATTHANA-SUTTA, *translated by Thich Nhat Hanh and Annabel Laity*

# PITH OF THE MATTER

SUPPOSE, friends, a person in need of sound timber, in quest of sound timber, going about searching for sound timber, should come upon a mighty tree, upstanding, all sound timber, and pass it by; but should cut away the outer wood and bark and take that only, thinking it to be sound timber.

Then another, more discerning person might say, "This person surely cannot tell the difference between sound timber and outer wood and bark, branch-wood and twigs; but being in need of sound timber this person passes it by and goes off with the outer wood and bark, thinking it to be sound timber. Now, such a way of dealing with sound timber will never serve this person's needs.

Thus, friends, the essentials of the holy life do not consist in the profits of gain, honor, and good name; nor even in the profits of observing moral rules; nor even in the profits of knowledge and insight; but the sure heart's release, friends—that, friends, is the meaning, that is the essence, that is the goal of living the holy life.

*adapted from the* MAJJHIMA NIKAYA,
*translated by F. L. Woodward*

# RADIANT PRESENCE

However young,
The seeker who sets out upon the way
Shines bright over the world.

But day and night
The person who is awake
Shines in the radiance of the spirit.

Meditate.
Live purely.
Be quiet.
Do your work, with mastery.

Like the moon,
Come out from behind the clouds!
Shine.

*from the* DHAMMAPADA,
*translated by Thomas Byrom*

# BAHIYA

THEN, Bahiya, thus must you train yourself: In the seen there will be just the seen, in the heard just the heard, in the sensed just the sensed, in the imagined just the imagined. Thus you will have no "thereby." That is how you must train yourself. Now, Bahiya, when in the seen there will be to you just the seen, in the heard just the heard, in the imagined just the imagined, in the cognized just the cognized, then, Bahiya, as you will have no "thereby," you will have no "therein." As you, Bahiya, will have no "therein," it follows that you will have no "here" or "beyond" or "midway between." That is just the end of Ill.

*adapted from the* UDANA,
*translated by F. L. Woodward*

# SUTRA ON FULL
# AWARENESS OF BREATHING

WHEN the full moon day arrived, the Buddha, seated under the open sky, looked over the assembly and said:

"O followers of the way, the method of being fully aware of breathing, if developed and practiced continuously, will have great rewards and bring great advantages. It will lead to success in the practice of the Seven Factors of Awakening. The Seven Factors of Awakening, if developed and practiced continuously, will give rise to Understanding and Liberation of the Mind.

"What is the way to develop and practice continuously the method of Full Awareness of Breathing so that the practice will be rewarding and offer great benefit?

"It is like this, the practitioner goes into the forest or to the foot of a tree, or to any deserted place, and sits stably in the cross-legged position, holding one's body quite straight. Breathing in, one knows that one is breathing in; and breathing out, one knows that one is breathing out.

"Breathing in a long breath, one knows, 'I am breathing in a long breath.' Breathing out a long breath, one knows, 'I am breathing out a long breath.'

"Breathing in a short breath, one knows, 'I am breathing in a short breath.' Breathing out a short breath, one knows, 'I am breathing out a short breath.'

"'I am breathing in and am aware of my whole body. I am breathing out and am aware of my whole body.' This is how one practices.

"'I am breathing in and making my whole body calm and at peace. I am breathing out and making my whole body calm and at peace.' This is how one practices.

"'I am breathing in and feeling joyful. I am breathing out and feeling joyful.' This is how one practices.

"'I am breathing in and feeling happy. I am breathing out and feeling happy.' One practices like this.

"'I am breathing in and am aware of the activities of the mind in me. I am breathing out and am aware of the activities of the mind in me.' One practices like this.

"'I am breathing in and making the activities of the mind in me calm and at peace. I am breathing out and making the activities of the mind in me calm and at peace.' One practices like this.

"'I am breathing in and am aware of my mind. I am breathing out and am aware of my mind.' One practices like this.

"'I am breathing in and making my mind happy and at peace. I am breathing out and making my mind happy and at peace.' One practices like this.

"'I am breathing in and concentrating my mind. I am breathing out and concentrating my mind.' One practices like this.

"'I am breathing in and liberating my mind. I am breathing out and liberating my mind.' One practices like this.

"'I am breathing in and observing the impermanent nature of all dharmas. I am breathing out and observing the impermanent nature of all dharmas.' One practices like this.

"'I am breathing in and observing the fading of all dharmas. I am breathing out and observing the fading of all dharmas.' One practices like this.

"'I am breathing in and contemplating liberation. I am breathing out and contemplating liberation.' One practices like this.

"'I am breathing in and contemplating letting go. I am breathing out and contemplating letting go.' One practices like this.

"The Full Awareness of Breathing, if developed and practiced continuously according to these instructions, will be rewarding and of great benefit."

*adapted from* THE SUTRA ON FULL AWARENESS OF BREATHING, *translated by Thich Nhat Hanh*

# THE HEART

FRIENDS, I know nothing which is as intractable as an untamed heart. The untamed heart is indeed intractable.

Friends, I know nothing which is as tractable as a tamed heart. The tamed heart is indeed tractable.

Friends, I know nothing which tends toward loss as does an untamed heart. Indeed, the untamed heart tends toward loss.

Friends, I know nothing which tends toward growth as does a tamed heart. Indeed, the tamed heart tends toward growth.

Friends, I know nothing which brings suffering as does an untamed, uncontrolled, unattended, and unrestrained heart. Such a heart brings suffering.

Friends, I know nothing which brings joy as does a tamed, controlled, attended, and restrained heart. Such a heart brings joy.

*from the* ANGUTTARA NIKAYA,
*translated by Gil Fronsdal*

# THE ABANDONING

## OF SORROW

THUS have I heard, once in the Jeta Grove the Buddha addressed the monks thus:

"Monks, I say that the elimination of the causes of sorrow is for one who knows and sees wisely, not for one who does not know and see wisely.

"Monks, there are causes of sorrow that should be abandoned by not paying attention to them. There are causes of sorrow that should be abandoned by restraining. There are causes of sorrow that should be abandoned by using. There are causes of sorrow that should be abandoned by enduring. There are causes of sorrow that should be abandoned by removing. There are causes of sorrow that should be abandoned by developing.

"What causes of sorrow should be abandoned by not paying attention to them? They are those things which, when dwelt upon, give rise to sorrow and which increase existing sorrow.

"Monks, a well-taught noble disciple, is skilled and disciplined in their Dharma, understands what things are fit for attention and what things are unfit for attention. Since that is so, such a person does not dwell upon to those things unfit for attention and attends to those things fit for attention.

"What causes of sorrow should be abandoned by restraining? Here a person, reflecting wisely, abides without wanting, with the senses restrained. While causes for sorrow, vexation, and fever might arise in one who is lost in sense experience, there are no causes of sorrow, vexation, and fever for the one who does not become lost in sense experience.

"What are the causes of sorrow that should be abandoned by using? Here a person, reflecting wisely, uses food neither for amusement nor for intoxication nor for the sake of physical beauty and attractiveness, but only for the endurance and continuance of this body, for ending discomfort, and for assisting the holy life, considering: 'Thus I shall complete old feelings without arousing new grasping and I shall be healthy and blameless and shall live in comfort.'

"Reflecting wisely, one uses one's resting place only for protection from cold, for protection from heat, for protection from insects, wind, the sun, creeping things, dangers, and for enjoying retreat.

"Reflecting wisely, one uses the medicinal requisites only for protection from arisen afflictions and for the benefit of good health.

"What causes of sorrow should be abandoned by enduring? Here a person, reflecting wisely, bears cold and heat, hunger and thirst, insects, wind, sun, and creeping things; one endures ill-spoken, unwelcome words. One bears bodily feelings that are painful, racking, sharp, piercing, disagreeable, and distressing. While causes of suffering, vexation, and fever may arise in one who does not endure such things, there are no causes of sorrow, vexation, and fever in one who endures them.

"What causes of sorrow should be abandoned by avoiding? Here a person, reflecting wisely, avoids a wild elephant, a wild horse, a wild bull, a wild dog, a snake, a stump, a bramble patch, a chasm, a cliff, a cesspit, and a sewer. Reflecting wisely, one avoids sitting on unsuitable seats, wandering to unsuitable resorts, and associating with bad friends. While causes of sorrow, vexation, and fever might arise in one who does not avoid these things, there are no causes of sorrow, vexation, and fever in one who avoids them.

"What causes of sorrow should be abandoned by removing? Here a person, reflecting wisely, does not tolerate an arisen thought of sensual desire; one abandons it, removes it, does away with it, and ends it. One does not tolerate an arisen thought of ill will. . . . One does not tolerate an arisen thought of cruelty. . . . One does not tolerate an arisen evil, or unwholesome states; one abandons them, releases them, does away with them and ends them. While causes of sorrow, vexation, and fever might arise in one who does not remove these thoughts, there is no taint, vexation, and fever in one who removes them.

"What causes of sorrow should be abandoned by developing? Here a person, reflecting wisely, develops mindfulness, investigation, energy, rapture, tranquillity, concentration, and equanimity. While causes of sorrow, vexation, and fever might arise in one who does not develop these, there are no causes of sorrow, vexation, or fever in one who develops them."

That is how the Buddha spoke. The monks were satisfied and delighted in the Blessed One's words.

*adapted from the* MAJJHIMA NIKAYA, *translated by Bhikkhu Nanamoli and Bhikkhu Bodhi*

# PARABLE OF THE LUTE

ONCE the Blessed One lived near Rajagaha, on Vulture Peak. At that time while the venerable Sona lived alone and secluded in the Cool Forest, this thought occurred to him:

"Of those disciples of the Blessed One who are energetic, I am one. Yet, my mind has not found freedom."

Now the Blessed One, perceiving in his own mind the venerable Sona's thoughts, left Vulture Peak, and, as speedily as a strong man might stretch his bent arm or bend his stretched arm, he appeared in the Cool Forest before the venerable Sona. And he said to the venerable Sona:

"Sona, did not this thought arise in your mind: 'Of those disciples of the Blessed One who are energetic, I am one. Yet, my mind has not found freedom.'"

"Yes, Lord."

"Tell me, Sona, in earlier days were you not skilled in playing string music on a lute?"

"Yes, Lord."

"And tell me, Sona, when the strings of your lute were too taut, was then your lute tuneful and easily playable?"

"Certainly not, O Lord."

"And when the strings of your lute were too loose, was then your lute tuneful and easily playable?"

"Certainly not, O Lord."

"But when, Sona, the strings of your lute were neither too taut nor too loose, but adjusted to an even pitch, did your lute then have a wonderful sound and was it easily playable?"

"Certainly, O Lord."

"Similarly, Sona, if energy is applied too strongly, it will lead to restlessness, and if energy is too lax it will lead to lassitude. Therefore, Sona, keep your energy in balance and balance the Spiritual Faculties and in this way focus your attention."

"Yes, O Lord," replied the venerable Sona in assent.

Afterward the venerable Sona kept his energy balanced, balanced the Spiritual Faculties and in this way focused his attention. And the venerable Sona, living alone and secluded, diligent, ardent and resolute, soon realized here and now, through his own direct knowledge, that unequaled goal of the holy life.

*adapted from the* ANGUTTARA NIKAYA,
*translated by Nyanaponika Thera*

# INCLINATION

# OF MIND

OTHERS will be cruel; we shall not be cruel. Thus, one should incline the mind.

Others will kill living beings; we shall abstain from killing living beings. Thus, one should incline the mind.

Others will take what is not given; we shall abstain from taking what is not given. Thus, one should incline the mind.

Others will engage in inappropriate sexuality; we shall abstain from inappropriate sexuality. Thus one should incline the mind.

Others will speak falsehoods; we shall abstain from false speech. Thus, one should incline the mind.

Others will speak maliciously; we shall abstain from malicious speech. Thus, one should incline the mind.

Others will gossip; we shall abstain from gossip. Thus, one should incline the mind.

Others will be envious; we shall not be envious. Thus, one should incline the mind.

Others will be avaricious; we shall not be avaricious.
   Thus, one should incline the mind.
Others will be fraudulent; we shall not be fraudulent.
   Thus, one should incline the mind.
Others will be arrogant; we shall not be arrogant.
   Thus, one should incline the mind.
Others will be unmindful; we shall be established in
   mindfulness. Thus, one should incline the mind.
Others will lack wisdom; we shall cultivate wisdom.
   Thus, one should incline the mind.

*adapted from the* MAJJHIMA NIKAYA,
*translated by Bhikkhu Nanamoli and Bhikkhu Bodhi*

# INNER PEACE

As in the ocean's midmost depth no wave is born,
but all is still, so let the practitioners be still, be
motionless, and nowhere should they swell.

*from the* SUTTA-NIPATA,
*translated by Dines Andersen and Helmer Smith*

# ABANDONING

# ALL HINDRANCES

"Endowed with this noble aggregate of moral discipline, this noble restraint over the sense faculties, this noble mindfulness and clear comprehension, and this noble contentment, a monk resorts to a secluded dwelling, sits down, crosses his legs, holds his body erect, and sets up mindfulness before him.

"Having abandoned covetousness for the world, he dwells with a mind free from covetousness; he purifies his mind from covetousness. Having abandoned ill will and hatred, he dwells with a benevolent mind, sympathetic for the welfare of all living beings; he purifies his mind from ill will and hatred. Having abandoned dullness and drowsiness, he dwells perceiving light, mindful, and clearly comprehending; he purifies his mind from dullness and drowsiness. Having abandoned restlessness and worry, he dwells at ease within himself, with a peaceful mind; he purifies his mind from restlessness and worry. Having abandoned doubt, he dwells as one who has passed beyond doubt, unperplexed about wholesome states; he purifies his mind from doubt.

"Suppose a man were to become sick, afflicted, gravely ill, so that he could not enjoy his food and his strength would decline. After some time he would recover from that illness and would enjoy his food and regain his bodily strength. He would reflect on this, and as a result he would become glad and experience joy.

"Again, suppose a man were a slave, without independence, subservient to others, unable to go where he wants. After some time he would be released from slavery and gain his independence; he would no longer be subservient to others but a free man able to go where he wants. He would reflect on this, and as a result he would become glad and experience joy.

"Again, suppose a man with wealth and possessions were traveling along a desert road where food was scarce and dangers were many. After some time he would cross over the desert and arrive safely at a village which is safe and free from danger. He would reflect on this, and as a result he would become glad and experience joy.

"When he sees that these five hindrances have been abandoned within himself, he regards that as freedom from debt, as good health, as release from prison, as freedom from slavery, as a place of safety."

*from the* DIGHA NIKAYA,
*translated by Bhikkhu Bodhi*

# SOMA AND MARA

ONCE the nun Soma, having returned from her alms round and after her meal, entered the woods for a noonday rest. Plunging into the depths of the woods, she sat down under a tree.

Then the tempter Mara, desirous of arousing fear, wavering, and dread in Soma, and wishing to cause her to interrupt her concentrated meditation, went up to her and said, "The goal is hard to reach, hard even for sages; it cannot be won by a woman with whatever wisdom she may have."

Then Soma thought, "Who is this, a human or a nonhuman, who is saying this? Surely it is the evil Mara who wants to interrupt my concentrated meditation." Knowing that it was Mara, she said to him, "What does one's gender matter to one whose mind is well-composed, in whom insight is functioning, and who comprehends the Dharma?"

Then the evil Mara thought, "The nun Soma knows me." Being sad and sorrowful, he vanished there and then.

*adapted from the* SAMYUTTA NIKAYA,
*translated by C. A. F. Rhys-Davids*

# SONGS OF THE NUNS

F REE woman,
be free
as the moon is freed
from the eclipse of the sun.

With a free mind,
in no debt,
enjoy what has been given to you.

Get rid of the tendency
to judge yourself
above, below, or
equal to others.
A nun who has self-possession
and integrity
will find the peace that nourishes
and never causes surfeit.

Be filled with all good things
like the moon on the fifteenth day.
Completely, perfectly full
of wisdom
tear open
the massive dark.

I, a nun, trained and self-composed,
established mindfulness
and entered peace like an arrow.
The elements of body and mind grew still,
happiness came.

Everywhere clinging to pleasure is destroyed,
the great dark is torn apart,
and Death,
you too are destroyed.

*from the* THERIGATHA,
*translated by Susan Murcott*

# LOOK WITHIN

THERE is no fire like greed,
    No crime like hatred,
No sorrow like separation,
No sickness like hunger of heart,
And no joy like the joy of freedom.

Health, contentment and trust
Are your greatest possessions,
And freedom your greatest joy.

Look within.
Be still.
Free from fear and attachment,
Know the sweet joy of living in the way.

*adapted from the* DHAMMAPADA,
*translated by Thomas Byrom*

# THE SHARPEST SWORD

O N a certain day when the Buddha dwelt at Jetavana, a celestial deva came to him in the shape of Brahman, whose countenance was bright and whose garments were white as snow.

The deva asked the Buddha, "What is the sharpest sword? What is the deadliest poison? What is the fiercest fire? What is the darkest night?"

The Buddha replied, "A word spoken in wrath is the sharpest sword; covetousness is the deadliest poison; hatred is the fiercest fire; ignorance is the darkest night."

The deva asked, "What is the greatest gain? What is the greatest loss? What armor is invulnerable? What is the best weapon?"

The Buddha replied, "The greatest gain is to give to others; the greatest loss is to receive without gratitude. Patience is an invulnerable armor; wisdom is the best weapon."

The deva asked, "Who is the most dangerous thief? What is the most precious treasure?"

The Buddha replied, "Unwholesome thought is the most dangerous thief; virtue is the most precious treasure."

The deva asked, "What is attractive? What is unpleasant? What is the most horrible pain? What is the greatest enjoyment?"

The Buddha replied, "Wholesomeness is attractive; unwholesomeness is unpleasant. A bad conscience is the most tormenting pain; awakening is the height of bliss."

The deva asked, "What causes ruin in the world? What breaks off friendships? What is the most violent fever? Who is the best physician?"

The Buddha replied, "Ignorance causes ruin in the world; envy and selfishness break off friendships; hatred is the most violent fever; the Buddha is the best physician."

The deva then continued, "Now I have only one doubt to be cleared away: What is it fire cannot burn, nor moisture corrode, nor wind crush down, but is able to benefit the whole world?"

The Buddha replied, "Blessing! Neither fire, nor moisture, nor wind can destroy the blessing of a good deed, and blessings benefit the whole world."

Hearing these answers, the deva was filled with joy. Bowing down in respect, he disappeared suddenly from the presence of the Buddha.

*from* THE GOSPEL OF THE BUDDHA *by Paul Carus*

# BAMBOO ACROBATS

O̲ N a certain occasion, the Exalted One was dwelling in the Sumbha country, in a township of the Sumbhas, called Sedaka. There the Exalted One addressed the monks:

"Once upon a time, monks, a bamboo-acrobat set up his pole and called to his pupil, Medakathalika, saying: 'Come, my lad, Medakathalika, climb the pole and stand on my shoulders!'

"'All right, master,' replied the pupil to the bamboo-acrobat. The student then climbed the pole and stood on his master's shoulder. Then, monks, the bamboo-acrobat said to his pupil: 'Now Medakathalika, my lad, you protect me well and I shall protect you. Thus watched and warded by each other, we will show our tricks, get a good fee, and come down safe from the bamboo-pole.'

"At these words Medakathalika the pupil said to the bamboo-acrobat: 'No, no! That won't do, master! You look after yourself, master, and I'll look after myself. Thus watched and warded each by himself, we'll show our tricks, get a good fee, and come down safe from the bamboo-pole.'

"Therein that is the right way," said the Exalted One, "Just as Medakathalika the pupil said to his master, 'I'll protect myself,' so, monks, should the Foundation of Mindfulness be practiced. 'I'll protect others': so should the Foundations of Mindfulness be practiced. Protecting oneself, monks, one protects others; protecting others, one protects oneself.

"And how, monks, does one, in protecting oneself, protect others? By frequent practice, development, and making much of the Foundations of Mindfulness. Thus, monks, in protecting oneself one protects others.

"And how, monks, does one, in protecting others, protect oneself? By forbearance, by nonviolence, by loving-kindness, by compassion. Thus, monks, in protecting others, one protects onself.

"'I shall protect myself': with this intention, monks, the Foundations of Mindfulness should be practiced. 'I shall protect others': with this intention the Foundations of Mindfulness should be practiced. Protecting oneself, one protects others; protecting others, one protects oneself."

*adapted from the* SAMYUTTA NIKAYA,
*translated by John Ireland*

# BLESSING CHANT

J ust as water flowing in the streams and rivers fills the ocean, thus may all your moments of goodness touch and benefit all beings, those here now and those gone before.

May all your wishes be soon fulfilled as completely as the moon on a full-moon night, as successfully as from the Wish-Fulfilling Gem. May all dangers be averted; may all disease leave you.

May no obstacles come across your way and may you enjoy happiness and long life.

May those who are always respectful, honoring the way of the elders, prosper in the four blessings of old age, beauty, happiness, and strength.

*adapted from the* PATTANUMODANA *blessing chant*

# PARABLE OF THE RAFT

"MONKS, I will teach you the parable of the raft—for getting across, not for retaining. It is like a man who going on a journey sees a great stretch of water, the near bank with dangers and fears, the farther bank secure and without fears, but there is neither a boat for crossing over, nor a bridge across. It occurs to him that to cross over from the perils of this bank to the security of the farther bank, he should fashion a raft out of sticks and branches and depending on the raft, cross over to safety. When he has done this it occurs to him that the raft has been very useful and he wonders if he ought to take it with him on his head or shoulders. What do you think, monks? That the man is doing what should be done to the raft?"

"No, lord."

"What should that man do, monks? When he has crossed over to the beyond he must leave the raft and proceed on his journey. Monks, a man doing this would be doing what should be done to the raft. In this way I have taught you Dharma, like the parable of the raft, for getting across, not for retaining. You, monks, by understanding the parable of the raft, must not cling to right states of mind and, all the more, to wrong states of mind."

*adapted from the* MAJJHIMA NIKAYA,
*translated by Christmas Humphreys*

# THE KALAMAS'S

# DILEMMA

ONE time Buddha was walking on tour with a large group of monks, when he came to a town of the Kalamas called Kesaputta.

The Kalamas of Kesaputta thought: "It is very good indeed to see Awakened Ones such as these." And so they went up to where Buddha was. Having seated themselves to one side, the Kalamas of Kesaputta said this to Buddha:

"There are, sir, many different teachers that come to Kesaputta. They illustrate and illuminate their own doctrines, but the doctrines of others they put down, revile, disparage, and cripple. For us, sir, uncertainty arises, and doubts arise concerning them: Who indeed of these venerable teachers speaks truly, who speaks falsely?"

"It is indeed fitting, Kalamas, to be uncertain, it is fitting to doubt. For in situations of uncertainty, doubts surely arise. You should decide, Kalamas, not by what you have heard, not by following convention, not by assuming it is so, not by relying on the texts, not because of reasoning, not because of logic, not by thinking about explanations, not by acquiescing to the views that you prefer, not because it appears likely, and certainly not out of respect for a teacher.

"When you would know, Kalamas, for *yourselves*, that 'These things are unhealthy, these things, when entered upon and undertaken, incline toward harm and suffering'—then, Kalamas, you should reject them.

"What do you think, Kalamas? When greed, hatred, or delusion arise within a person, does it arise for their welfare or their harm?"

"For their harm, sir."

"And when a person has become greedy, hateful, or deluded, their mind consumed by this greed, hatred, or delusion, Kalamas, do they kill living creatures, and take what has not been given, and go to another's spouse, and speak what is false, and induce others to undertake what is, for a long time, to their harm and suffering?"

"This is true, sir."

"And what do you think, Kalamas? Are these things healthy or unhealthy?"

"Unhealthy, sir."

"And when entered upon and undertaken, do they incline toward harm and suffering or don't they?"

"We agree, sir, that they do."

"But when you would know, Kalamas, for *yourselves*, that 'These things are healthy, these things, when entered upon and undertaken, incline toward welfare and happiness'—then, Kalamas, having come to them you should stay with them.

"What do you think, Kalamas? When nongreed, nonhatred, or nondelusion arise within a person, does it arise for their welfare or their harm?"

"For their welfare, sir."

"And when a person has not become greedy, hateful, or deluded, their mind not consumed by this greed, hatred, or delusion, Kalamas, do they not kill living creatures, and not take what has not been given, and not go to another's spouse, and not speak what is false, and induce others to undertake what is, for a long time, to their welfare and happiness?"

"This is true, sir."

"And what do you think, Kalamas? Are these things healthy or unhealthy?"

"Healthy, sir."

"And when entered upon and undertaken, do they incline toward welfare and happiness or don't they?"

"We agree, sir, that they do."

"That person, Kalamas, who is a follower of the noble path is thus free of wanting, free of harming, and without confusion. Clearly conscious and mindful, he or she abides having suffused the first direction, then the second, then the third and fourth—and so above, below, and across, everywhere and in every way—with a mind dedicated to loving kindness, compassion, good will, and equanimity that is abundant, expansive, immeasurable, kindly, and free of harming.

"And so, Kalamas, the follower of the noble path whose mind is thus kindly and free of harming—their mind is not defiled, but is purified."

*adapted from the* ANGUTTARA NIKAYA,
*translated by Andy Olendzki*

# PATIENCE

AT one time Shakyamuni Buddha was staying in the town of Kosambi. In this town there was one who resented him and who bribed wicked men to circulate false stories about him. Under these circumstances it was difficult for his disciples to get sufficient food from their begging, and there was much abuse.

Ananda said to Shakyamuni, "We had better not stay in a town like this. There are other and better towns to go to. We had better leave this town."

The Blessed One replied, "Suppose the next town is like this, what shall we do then?"

"Then we move to another."

The Blessed One said, "No, Ananda, there will be no end in that way. We had better remain here and bear the abuse patiently until it ceases and then move to another place. There are profit and loss, slander and honor, praise and blame, pain and pleasure in this world; the Enlightened One is not controlled by these external things; they will cease as quickly as they come."

*adapted from the* DHAMMAPADA ATTHAKATHA,
*translated by Bukkyo Dendo Kyokai*

# CRITICISM AND PRAISE

THE Buddha said: "If outsiders speak against me, the Teaching, or the Order, you should not be angry for that would prevent your own self-conquest. Similarly if they praise us. But you should find out what is false or true, and acknowledge the fact. And even in praise it is only of trifling matters that an unconverted man might speak of me."

*from the* DIGHA NIKAYA, *translated by C. A. F. Rhys-Davids*

# ON CONFLICT

# AND CONCORD

THE venerable Shariputra asked the Buddha, "How am I to behave, O Lord, toward those in conflict?"

"Do not reprove them, Shariputra," said the Blessed One, "for harsh words do not serve as a remedy and are pleasant to no one. Assign them to separate dwelling-places and treat them with impartial justice. Listen with patience to both parties. Only the person who weighs both sides is called a sage. When both parties have presented their case, let the community come to an agreement and declare the re-establishment of concord.

"There are two ways of re-establishing concord: one is in the letter, and the other one is in the spirit and in the letter.

"If the community declares the re-establishment of concord without having inquired into the matter, the peace is concluded in the letter only. But if the community, having inquired into the matter and having gone to the bottom of it, decides to declare the re-establishment of concord, the peace is concluded in the spirit and also in the letter.

"The concord re-established in the spirit and in the letter is alone right and lawful."

*from* THE GOSPEL OF THE BUDDHA *by Paul Carus*

# ADMONISHING OTHERS

ONE who is about to admonish another must realize within herself or himself five qualities before doing so. [He or she must intend] thus:

"In due season will I speak, not out of season. In truth will I speak, not in falsehood. Gently will I speak, not harshly. To one's profit will I speak, not to one's loss. With kindly intent will I speak, not in anger."

*adapted from the* VINAYA PITAKA,
*translated by F. L. Woodward*

# CONCEIT OF VIEWS

THE Buddha said, "To be attached to a certain view and to look down upon other views as inferior—this the wise call a fetter."

*from the* SUTTA NIPATA, *translated by K. R. Norman*

# RIGHT SPEECH

*Abstaining from Lying*

Herein someone avoids lying and abstains from it. One speaks the truth, is devoted to the truth, reliable, worthy of confidence, not a deceiver of others. Being at a meeting, or among people, or in the midst of relatives, or in society, or in the king's court, and called upon and asked as witness to tell what one knows, one answers, if one knows nothing: "I know nothing," and if one knows, one answers: "I know"; if one has seen nothing, one answers: "I have seen nothing," and if one has seen, one answers: "I have seen." Thus one never knowingly speaks a lie, either for the sake of one's own advantage, or for the sake of another person's advantage, or for the sake of any advantage whatsoever.

*Abstaining from Tale-Bearing*

One avoids tale-bearing and abstains from it. What one has heard here, one does not repeat there, so as to cause dissension there; and what one has heard there, one does not repeat here, so as to cause dissension here. Thus one unites those that are divided; and those that are united, one encourages. Concord gladdens one, one delights and rejoices in concord; and it is concord that one spreads by one's words.

## Abstaining from Harsh Language

One avoids harsh language and abstains from it. One speaks such words as are gentle, soothing to the ear, loving, such words as go to the heart, and are courteous, friendly, and agreeable to many.

## Abstaining from Vain Talk

One avoids vain talk and abstains from it. One speaks at the right time, in accordance with facts, speaks what is useful, speaks of the law and the discipline; one's speech is like a treasure, uttered at the right moment, accompanied by understanding, moderate, and full of sense.

This is called Right Speech.

*adapted from the* ANGUTTARA NIKAYA,
*translated by Nyanatiloka*

# VALUE OF

# LOVING-KINDNESS

"NONE of the means employed to acquire religious merit, O monks, has a sixteenth part of the value of loving-kindness. Loving-kindness, which is freedom of heart, absorbs them all; it glows, it shines, it blazes forth.

"And in the same way, O monks, as the light of all the stars has not a sixteenth part of the value of the moonlight, but the moonlight absorbs it and glows and shines and blazes forth: in the same way, O monks, none of the means employed to acquire religious merit has a sixteenth part of the value of loving-kindness. Loving-kindness, which is freedom of heart, absorbs them; it glows, it shines, it blazes forth.

"And in the same way, O monks, as at the end of the rainy season, the sun, rising into the clear and cloudless sky, banishes all the dark spaces and glows and shines and blazes forth: in the same way again, as at night's end the morning star glows and shines and blazes forth: so, O monks, none of the means employed to acquire religious merit has a sixteenth part of the value of loving-kindness. Loving-kindness, which is freedom of heart, absorbs them: it glows, it shines, it blazes forth."

*adapted from the* ITIVUTTAKA, *translated by Justin H. Moore*

# THE WOMAN
# AT THE WELL

ANANDA, the attendant to the Buddha, having been sent by the Lord on a mission, passed by a well near a village, and seeing Pakati, a young outcast woman, asked her for water to drink.

Pakati said, "O monk, I am too humbly born to give you water to drink. Do not ask any service of me lest your holiness be contaminated, for I am of low caste."

And Ananda replied, "I ask not for caste but for water;" and the woman's heart leaped joyfully and she gave Ananda water to drink.

Ananda thanked her and went away; but she followed him at a distance.

Having heard that Ananda was a disciple of the Buddha, the woman went to the Blessed One and said, "O Lord, help me and let me live in the place where your disciple Ananda dwells, so that I may see him and minister unto him, for I love Ananda."

And the Blessed One understood the emotions of her heart and he said, "Pakati, your heart is full of love, but you do not understand your own sentiments. It is not Ananda that you love, but his kindness. Accept, then, the kindness you have seen him practice toward you and practice it toward others.

"Pakati, though you are born low caste, you will be a model for noblemen and noblewomen. Swerve not from the path of justice and righteousness and you will outshine the royal glory of queens and kings."

*adapted from the* AGAMAS,
*translated by E. Burneuf and P. Carus*

# TREASURE

A WOMAN buries a treasure in a deep pit, thinking: "It will be useful in time of need, or if the king is displeased with me, or if I am robbed or fall into debt, or if food is scarce, or bad luck befalls me."

But all this treasure may not profit the owner at all, for she may forget where she has hidden it, or goblins may steal it, or her enemies or even her kinsmen may take it when she is careless.

But by charity, goodness, restraint, and self-control man and woman alike can store up a well-hidden treasure—a treasure which cannot be given to others and which robbers cannot steal. A wise person should do good—that is the treasure which will not leave one.

*adapted from the* KHUDDHAKA PATHA, *translated by A. L. Basham*

# COMMITMENT TO VIRTUE

IF anyone with a pure heart undertakes a commitment to virtue—to refrain from taking life, from taking what is not given, from sexual immorality, from lying speech, and from taking strong drink and sloth-producing drugs—that constitutes a sacrifice better than giving alms, better than giving shelter, and better than going for refuge.

*adapted from the* DIGHA NIKAYA,
*translated by Maurice Walshe*

# THE FIVE PRECEPTS

1. For the purpose of training I vow to refrain from taking life.
2. For the purpose of training I vow to refrain from taking what is not given.
3. For the purpose of training I vow to refrain from sexual misconduct.
4. For the purpose of training I vow to refrain from false speech.
5. For the purpose of training I vow to refrain from intoxicants which lead to carelessness.

These Five Precepts are a vehicle of happiness, a vehicle of good fortune, a vehicle for liberation. Let our virtue therefore be purified and shine forth.

*translated by Gil Fronsdal*

# TENDING THE SICK

Now, at that time a certain monk was suffering from dysentery and lay where he had fallen down in his own excrements.

And as the Buddha was walking about he came to the lodging of that monk. When he saw that monk lying where he had fallen in his own excrements, he went over to him and said, "Brother, what ails you?"

"I have dysentery, Lord."

"But is there anyone taking care of you, brother?"

"No, Lord."

"Why is it, brother, that the monks do not take care of you?"

"I am useless to the monks, Lord, therefore the monks do not take care of me."

Then the Buddha said to the venerable Ananda, "Go, Ananda, and fetch water. We will wash this brother."

When Ananda had fetched the water, the Buddha poured it out, while the venerable Ananda washed that brother all over. Then the Buddha taking him by the head and the venerable Ananda taking him by the feet, together they laid him on the bed.

Then the Buddha, in this connection and on this occasion, gathered the order of monks together, and questioned them, saying, "Monks, is there in such and such a lodging a brother who is sick?"

"There is, Lord."

"And what ails that brother?"

"Lord, that brother has dysentery."

"But, brethren, is there anyone taking care of him?"

"No, Lord."

"Why not? Why do the monks not take care of him?"

"That brother is useless to the order of monks, Lord. That is why the monks do not take care of him."

"Monks, you have no mother and no father to take care of you. If you will not take care of each other, who else will do so? Monks, those who would attend to me, let them attend to the sick."

*adapted from the* VINAYA PITAKA,

*translated by F. L. Woodward*

# WISE HOUSEHOLDERS

THE wise who are trained and disciplined
  Shine out like beacon lights
They earn money just as a bee
Gathers honey without harming the flowers,
And they let it grow as an anthill slowly gains in
    height.
With wealth wisely gained
They use it for the benefit of all.

*adapted from the* DIGHA NIKAYA,
*translated by Gil Fronsdal*

# ADVICE FOR SUSTAINING
# THE COMMUNITY

As long as the followers of the way hold regular and frequent assemblies, they may be expected to prosper and not decline. As long as they meet in harmony, break up in harmony, and carry on their business in harmony, they may be expected to prosper and not decline. As long as they do not authorize what has not been authorized already, and do not abolish what has been authorized, but proceed according to what has been authorized by the rules of training; as long as they honor, respect, revere, and salute the elders of long standing who are long ordained, fathers and leaders of the order; as long as they do not fall prey to desires which arise in them and lead to rebirth; as long as they are devoted to forest lodgings; as long as they preserve their personal mindfulness, so that in the future the good who are among their companions will come to them, and those who have already come will feel at ease with them; as long as the followers of the way hold to these seven things and are seen to do so, they may be expected to prosper and not decline.

*adapted from the* MAHAPARINIBBANA SUTTA,
*translated by Maurice Walshe*

# KNOWING A BETTER
# WAY TO LIVE

I HEARD these words of the Buddha one time when the Lord was staying at the monastery in the Jeta Grove, in the town of Sravasti. He called all the monks to him and instructed them, "Monks!"

And the monks replied, "We are here."

The Blessed One taught, "I will teach you what is meant by 'knowing the better way to live alone.' Monks, please listen carefully."

"Blessed One, we are listening."

The Buddha taught:

> "Do not pursue the past.
> Do not lose yourself in the future.
> The past no longer is.
> The future has not yet come.
> Looking deeply at life as it is
> in the very here and now,
> the practitioner dwells
> in stability and freedom.
> We must be diligent today.
> To wait until tomorrow is too late.

Death comes unexpectedly.
How can we bargain with it?
The sage calls a person who knows
how to dwell in mindfulness
night and day
'one who knows
the better way to live alone.'"

*adapted from the* BHADDEKARATTA SUTTA,
*translated by Thich Nhat Hanh*

# FREE FROM ALL OPINION

"THIS I do now declare, after investigation there is nothing among all doctrines that such a one as I would embrace. Seeing misery in philosophical views, without adopting any of them, searching for truth I discovered 'inward peace.'

"Not by any philosophical opinion, not by tradition, not by knowledge, not by virtue and holy works can anyone say that purity exists; nor by absence of philosophical opinion, by absence of tradition, by absence of knowledge, by absence of virtue and holy works either; having abandoned these without adopting anything else, let one, calm and independent, not desire any resting place.

"One who thinks oneself equal to others, or superior, or inferior, for that very reason disputes; but one who is unmoved under those three conditions, for that person the notions 'equal,' 'superior,' and 'inferior' do not exist.

"The Sage for whom the notions 'equal' and 'unequal' do not exist, would he say, 'This is true'? Or with whom should he dispute, saying, 'This is false'? With whom should he enter into dispute?

"An accomplished person does not by a philosophical view or by thinking become arrogant, for he is not of that sort; not by holy works, nor by tradition is he led, he is not led into any of the resting places of the mind.

"For one who is free from views there are no ties, for one who is delivered by understanding there are no follies; but those who grasp after views and philosophical opinions, they wander about in the world annoying people."

*adapted from the* SUTTA-NIPATA,
*translated by V. Fausböll*

# DO NOT GRASP AT VIEWS

Do not form views in the world through either knowledge, virtuous conduct, or religious observances; likewise, avoid thinking of oneself as being either superior, inferior, or equal to others.

The wise let go of the 'self' and being free of attachments they depend not on knowledge. Nor do they dispute opinions or fix upon any view.

For those who have no wishes for either extreme of becoming or non-becoming, here or in another existence, there is no conflict with the views held by others.

They do not form the least notion in regard to views seen, heard, or thought out. How could one influence those wise ones who do not grasp at any views.

*from the* SUTTA-NIPATA,
*translated by Gil Fronsdal*

# JUDGING ANOTHER

ONE evening, the Buddha arose from his meditation and was seated outside the eastern gate of the park where he was staying. Then, King Pasenadi, arriving for a visit, greeted the Buddha and took a seat to one side. Just at that time, not so far away, a large group of wandering ascetics were walking by. Carrying their alms bowls, some of these ascetics wore long matted hair, some were naked, some wore only a single robe, and some were wanderers. When they had passed by, the king asked the Buddha, "Can any of those ascetics be considered as being either arhats or on the path to arhatship?"

The Buddha responded, "It is by living a life in common with a person that we learn of that person's moral character; and then only if having insight ourselves, we have watched a person for a long time. It is only in conversation with a person that we learn of that person's wisdom and clarity of heart; and then only if, having insight ourselves, we have paid attention for a long time. It is during times of trouble that we learn of another's fortitude; and then only if, having insight ourselves, we have paid careful attention for a long time."

*adapted from the* SAMYUTTA NIKAYA,
*translated by Gil Fronsdal*

# A LAMP UNTO YOURSELF

THEREFORE, Ananda, be ye lamps unto yourselves, be ye a refuge to yourselves. Betake yourselves to no external refuge. Hold fast to the Truth as a lamp; hold fast to the Truth as a refuge. Look not for a refuge in anyone beside yourselves. And those, Ananda, who either now or after I am dead shall be a lamp unto themselves, shall betake themselves to no external refuge, but holding fast to the Truth as their lamp, and holding fast to the Truth as their refuge, shall not look for refuge to anyone beside themselves—it is they who shall reach the very topmost Height. But they must be anxious to learn.

*from the* MAHAPARINIBBANA SUTTA,
*translated by T. W. Rhys-Davids*

# LIVING IN THE WORLD

*by Ashvaghosha*

THE Dharma of the Buddha does not require a person to go into homelessness or to resign from the world, unless he or she feels called upon to do so; but the Dharma of the Buddha requires every person to free themselves from the illusion of self, to cleanse one's heart, to give up one's thirst for pleasure, and lead a life of righteousness.

And whatever people do, whether they remain in the world as artisans, merchants, or officers of the king, or retire from the world and devote themselves to a life of religious meditation, let them put their whole heart into their task; let them be diligent and energetic. And if, like the lotus flower, which grows out of muddy water but remains untouched by the mud, they engage in life without cherishing envy or hatred, and if they live in the world not a life of self but a life of truth, then surely joy, peace, and bliss will dwell in their minds.

*adapted from the* BUDDHACARITA, *translated by Samuel Beal*

# GO FORTH OVER
# THE EARTH

ONCE the Buddha addressed his awakened followers, "My friends, I am free of all human and
divine entanglements. And as you are likewise free of
all human and divine entanglements, go forth into the
world for the good of the many, for the happiness of
the many, with compassion for the world, and for the
benefit, the blessing, and the happiness of gods and
humans. Do not two of you go out on the same road.
Teach Dharma that is good in the beginning, in the
middle, and in the end. Reveal the spiritual life, complete and pure in spirit and in form."

*from the* SAMYUTTA NIKAYA,
*translated by Gil Fronsdal*

# LIKE MILK AND WATER

ONE evening the Buddha rose from meditation and went to the Park of the Gosinga Sala-tree Wood. The park keeper saw the Buddha coming and told him, "Do not enter this park, recluse. There are three clansmen here seeking their own good. Do not disturb them."

The venerable Anuruddha heard the park keeper speaking to the Buddha and told him, "Friend park keeper, do not keep the Buddha out. It is our Teacher who has come." Then the venerable Anuruddha went to the venerable Nandiya and the venerable Kimbila and said, "Come out, venerable sirs, come out! Our Teacher has come."

Then all three went to meet the Buddha. One took his bowl and outer robe, one prepared a seat, and one set out water for washing the feet. The Buddha sat down on the seat made ready and washed his feet. Then those three venerable ones paid homage to the Buddha and sat down to one side. When they were seated, the Buddha said to them, "I hope you are all keeping well. I hope you are all comfortable. I hope you have no trouble getting almsfood. I hope that you are living in concord, with mutual appreciation, without disputing, blending like milk and water, viewing each other with kindly eyes."

Anuruddha replied, "Surely, venerable sir, we are living in concord, with mutual appreciation, without disputing, blending like milk and water, viewing each other with kindly eyes."

"But how do you live thus?"

"Venerable sir, as to that, I think thus: 'It is a gain for me, it is great gain for me, that I am living with such companions in the holy life.' I maintain bodily acts of loving-kindness towards those venerable ones both openly and privately; I maintain verbal acts of loving-kindness towards them both openly and privately; I maintain mental acts of loving-kindness towards them both openly and privately. I consider, 'Why should I not set aside what I wish to do and do what these venerable ones wish to do.' Then I set aside what I wish to do and do what these venerable ones wish to do. We are different in body, venerable sir, but one in mind."

The venerable Nandiya and the venerable Kimbila each spoke likewise, adding: "That is how, venerable sir, we are living in concord, with mutual appreciation, without disputing, blending like milk and water, viewing each other with kindly eyes."

*from the* MAJJHIMA NIKAYA,
*translated by Bhikkhu Nanamoli and Bhikkhu Bodhi*

# SHARING BLESSINGS

By the blessings that have arisen from my
practice, may my Venerable Preceptors,
And Teachers who have helped me, Mother, Father
and relatives,
King and Queen, worldly powers, virtuous human
beings,
The Supreme Beings, Demons and High Gods, the
guardian deities of the world, celestial beings,
The Lord of Death; people—friendly, indifferent,
and hostile—
May all beings be well! May the skillful deeds done
by me,
Bring you three-fold bliss. May this quickly bring you
to the Deathless.
By this act of goodness and through the act of sharing,
May I likewise attain the cutting-off of craving and
clinging.
Whatever faults I have until I attain liberation,
May they quickly perish. Wherever I am born, may
there be
An upright mind, mindfulness and wisdom, austerity
and vigor.
May harmful influences not weaken my efforts.

The Buddha is the unexcelled protector, the Dharma
is the supreme protection,
Peerless is the "Silent Buddha," the Sangha is my true
refuge.
By the power of these Supreme Ones, may I rise
above all ignorance.

*from* REFLECTIONS ON SHARING BLESSINGS,
*translated by the Amaravati Buddhist Centre*

# THE DHARMA IS LIKE
# THE OCEAN

THE Dharma is like the ocean, having the same eight wonderful qualities. Both the ocean and the teachings become gradually deeper. Both preserve their identity under all changes. Both cast out dead bodies upon the dry land. As the great rivers, when falling into the sea, lose their names and are thenceforth reckoned as the great ocean, so all the castes, having renounced their lineage and entered the Order become equals and are reckoned in the family of the Buddha. The ocean is the goal of all streams and of the rain from the clouds, yet is it never overflowing and never emptier: so the Dharma is embraced by many millions of people, yet it neither increases nor decreases. As the great ocean has only one taste, the taste of salt, so the teachings have only one flavor, the flavor of emancipation. Both the ocean and the Dharma are full of gems and pearls, and both afford a dwelling-place for magnanimous beings. These are the eight wonderful qualities in which the Dharma resembles the ocean.

*from the* CULLAVAGGA, *translated by T. W. Rhys-Davids*

# ALL THINGS

# CONDITIONED

All things conditioned are unstable,
impermanent,
  Fragile in essence, as an unbaked pot,
Like something borrowed, or a city founded on sand,
  They last a short while only.

They are inevitably destroyed,
  Like plaster washed off in the rains,
Like the sandy bank of a river—
  They are conditioned, and their true nature is frail.

They are like the flame of a lamp,
  Which rises suddenly and as soon goes out.
They have no power of endurance, like the wind
  Or like foam, unsubstantial, essentially feeble.

The sage knows the beginning and end
  Of consciousness, its production and passing
  away—
The sage knows that it came from nowhere and
  returns to nowhere,
  And is empty of reality, like a conjuring trick.

The sage knows what is true reality,
    And sees all conditioned things as empty and
    powerless.

*adapted from the* LALITAVISTARA,
                    *translated by A. L. Basham*

# THE EYE OF WISDOM

THE Buddha said:

"I consider the positions of kings and rulers as that of dust motes in a sunbeam. I see the treasures of gold and gems as broken tiles. I look upon the finest silken robes as tattered rags. I see the myriad worlds of the universe as small seeds and the great Indian ocean as drops of mud that soil one's feet. I perceive the teachings of the world to be the illusions of magicians. I look upon the judgement of right and wrong as the serpentine dance of dragons, and the rise and fall of beliefs as the traces left by the four seasons."

*adapted from the* SUTRA OF FORTY-TWO SECTIONS,
*translated by Samuel Beal*

# HEART SUTRA

Thus have I heard at one time. The Buddha dwelt at Vulture Peak together with a sangha of one hundred thousand monks and nuns, and seventy thousand bodhisattvas. At that time the bodhisattva Avalokitesvara arose from her seat among the assembly and went up to the Buddha. Facing him she joined her palms together and bowed respectfully. With reverence she said, "I wish to explain for this assembly the bodhisattva's Heart of Perfect Wisdom which is the Universal Womb of Wisdom."

Then the Buddha said, "Excellent, excellent, Great Compassionate One!"

Then Avalokitesvara entered into her meditation and coursing in Perfect Wisdom observed that all five aggregates are empty of own-nature. Arising from her meditation she said:

"The nature of form is empty, emptiness is form. Form is not different from emptiness, emptiness is not different from form. That which is form is empty, that which is emptiness is form. Feelings, perceptions, mental formations, and consciousness are also like this. The nature of consciousness is empty, emptiness is consciousness. Consciousness is not different from emptiness, emptiness is not different from consciousness. That which is conciousness is empty, that which is emptiness is consciousness.

"These dharmas are marked with emptiness, neither arising nor ceasing, neither tainted nor pure, neither increasing nor decreasing. Therefore in emptiness there is no form, no feelings, no perceptions, no mental formations, no consciousness, no eye, ear, nose, taste, or touch; no realm of eyes and so on up to no realm of mind-consciousness; no ignorance and no extinction of ignorance, and so on up to no old age and death and also no extinction of old age and death; no suffering, no origin of suffering, no end to suffering, no path, no wisdom, and also no attainment.

"With nothing to attain the bodhisattvas depend on Perfect Wisdom and their minds are without any hindrance. Without any hindrance no fears exist. Far removed from perverted thought they are awake. All the Buddhas in the past, present, and future depend on Perfect Wisdom in attaining their unsurpassed complete and perfect awakening.

"Therefore, know the Perfection of Wisdom is the great mantra, is the bright mantra, is the unsurpassed mantra, is the unequaled mantra that can remove all suffering, and is true not false.

"Therefore proclaim the Perfect Wisdom mantra. Proclaim the mantra that says:

"GATE, GATE, PARAGATE, PARASAMGATE, BODHI, SVAHA!"

THE HEART SUTRA, *translated by Gil Fronsdal*

# THE DHARMA
# OF THE HEART

*by Huang Po*

By the Dharma is meant the heart, for there is no Dharma apart from heart. Heart is no other than the Dharma, for there is no heart apart from the Dharma. This heart in itself is empty, and there is no such empty heart either. When the empty heart is sought after by the heart, this is making it a particular object of thought. There is only testimony of silence, it goes beyond thinking. Therefore it is said that the Dharma cuts off the passage to words and puts an end to all forms of mental activities.

The heart is the source, the pure Buddha-nature that is inherent in all of us. All sentient beings, however mean and degraded, are not in this particular respect different from Buddhas and bodhisattvas—they are all of one substance. Only because of their imagination and false discrimination, sentient beings work out their karma and reap its result, while in their Buddha-nature itself there is nothing corresponding to it. The essence is empty and allows everything to pass through; it is quiet and at rest, it is illuminating, it is peaceful and productive of bliss. When you have within yourself a deep insight into this, you immediately realize that all that you need is there in perfection and in abundance, and nothing is at all wanting or lacking in you.

*adapted from* ON THE TRANSMISSION OF THE MIND,
*translated by John Blofeld*

# MIRAGE

THIS triple world resembles a net, or water in a mirage that is agitated; it is like a dream, *maya*; and by thus regarding it one is emancipated.

Like a mirage in the springtime, the mind is found bewildered; animals imagine water but there is no reality to it.

There is here nothing but thought construction, it is like an image in the air; when they thus understand all, there is nothing to know.

Eternity and non-eternity; oneness, too, bothness and not-bothness as well: these are discriminated by the ignorant who are confused in mind and bound up by errors since beginningless time.

In a mirror, in water, in an eye, in a vessel, and on a gem, images are seen; but in them there are no realities anywhere to take hold of.

*adapted from the* LANKAVATARA SUTRA,
*translated by D. T. Suzuki*

discrimination. But the elder Śāriputra has both constructual thought and discrimination.

"Reverend Śāriputra, impropriety for one who has renounced the world for the discipline of the rightly taught Dharma consists of constructual thought and discrimination, yet the elders are full of such thoughts. One who is without such thoughts is always proper.

"Reverend Śāriputra, see how these flowers do not stick to the bodies of these great spiritual heroes, the bodhisattvas! This is because they have eliminated constructual thoughts and discriminations.

"For example, evil spirits have power over fearful men but cannot disturb the fearless. Likewise, those intimidated by fear of the world are in the power of forms, sounds, smells, tastes, and textures, which do not disturb those who are free from fear of the passions inherent in the constructive world. Thus, these flowers stick to the bodies of those who have not eliminated their instincts for the passions and do not stick to the bodies of those who have eliminated their instincts. Therefore, the flowers do not stick to the bodies of these bodhisattvas, who have abandoned all instincts."

Śāriputra asked: Goddess, what prevents you from transforming yourself out of your female state?

The goddess replied: Although I have sought my "female state" for these twelve years, I have not yet found it. Reverend Śāriputra, if a magician were to incarnate a woman by magic, would you ask her, "What prevents you from transforming yourself out of your female state?"

*Śāriputra*: No! Such a woman would not really exist, so what would there be to transform?

*Goddess*: Just so, reverend Śāriputra, all things do not really exist. Now, would you think, "What prevents one whose nature is that of a magical incarnation from transforming herself out of her female state?"

Thereupon the goddess employed her magical power to cause the elder Śāriputra to appear in her form and to cause herself to appear in his form. Then the goddess, transformed into Śāriputra, said to Śāriputra, transformed into a goddess, "Reverend Śāriputra, what prevents you from transforming yourself out of your female state?"

And Śāriputra, transformed into the goddess, replied, "I no longer appear in the form of a male! My body has changed into the body of a woman! I do not know what to transform!"

The goddess continued, "If the elder could again change out of the female state, then all women could also change out of their female states. All women appear in the form of women in just the same way as the elder appears in the form of a woman. While they are not women in reality, they appear in the form of women. With this in mind, the Buddha said, 'In all things, there is neither male nor female.'"

Then, the goddess released her magical power and each returned to his ordinary form. She then said to him, "Reverend Śāriputra, what have you done with your female form?"

*Śāriputra*: I neither made it nor did I change it.

*Goddess*: Just so, all things are neither made nor changed, and that they are not made and not changed, that is the teaching of the Buddha.

*from the* VIMALAKIRTI SUTRA, *translated by Robert A. F. Thurman*

# FLEETING WORLD

Thus shall ye think of all this fleeting world:
 A star at dawn, a bubble in a stream;
A flash of lightning in a summer cloud,
A flickering lamp, a phantom, and a dream.

*from the* DIAMOND SUTRA,
*translated by A. F. Price*

# THE MIND OF THE
# ANCIENT BUDDHAS

*by Zen Master Dogen*

"THE mind of the ancient Buddhas" should not be understood as something irrelevant to your experience, as some mind which exists from the beginningless past, for it is the mind which eats rice gruel or tastes other food in your ordinary everyday life, it is the mind which is grass, the mind which is water. Within this life just as it is, is the act of sitting like a Buddha which is called "arousing the thought of enlightenment."

The conditions for arousing the thought of enlightenment do not come from anywhere else. It is the enlightened mind which arouses the thought of enlightenment. . . . One honors the Buddha with a grain of sand, one honors the Buddha with the water in which rice has been soaked. One offers a handful of food to living creatures.

*from* AROUSING THE SUPREME MIND,
*translated by Francis Cook*

# VERSES ON THE

# FAITH MIND

*by Seng-tsan*

THE Great Way is not difficult
for those who have no preferences.
When love and hate are both absent
everything becomes clear and undisguised.
Make the smallest distinction however
and heaven and earth are set infinitely apart.
If you wish to see the truth
then hold no opinions for or against anything.
To set up what you like against what you dislike is the
    disease of the mind.
When the deep meaning of things is not understood
the mind's essential peace is disturbed to no avail.

The Way is perfect like vast space
where nothing is lacking and nothing is in excess.
Indeed, it is due to our choosing to accept or reject
that we do not see the true nature of things.
Live neither in the entanglements of outer things,
nor in inner feelings of emptiness.
Be serene in the oneness of things

and such erroneous views will disappear by
    themselves.
When you try to stop activity to achieve passivity
your very effort fills you with activity.
As long as you remain in one extreme or the other
you will never know Oneness.

Those who do not live in the single Way
fail in both activity and passivity,
assertion and denial.
To deny the reality of things
is to miss their reality;
to assert the emptiness of things
is to miss their reality.
The more you talk and think about it,
the further astray you wander from the truth.
Stop talking and thinking,
and there is nothing you will not be able to know.
To return to the root is to find the meaning,
but to pursue appearances is to miss the source.
At the moment of inner enlightenment
there is a going beyond appearance and emptiness.
The changes that appear to occur in the empty world
we call real only because of our ignorance.
Do not search for the truth;
only cease to cherish opinions.

Do not remain in the dualistic state
avoid such pursuits carefully.
If there is even a trace
of this and that, of right and wrong,

the Mind-essence will be lost in confusion.
Although all dualities come from the One,
do not be attached even to this One.
When the mind exists undisturbed in the Way,
nothing in the world can offend,
and when a thing can no longer offend,
it ceases to exist in the old way.

When no discriminating thoughts arise,
the old mind ceases to exist.
When thought objects vanish,
the thinking-subject vanishes,
as when the mind vanishes, objects vanish.
Things are objects because of the subject [mind];
the mind [subject] is such because of things [object].
Understand the relativity of these two
and the basic reality: the unity of emptiness.
In this Emptiness the two are indistinguishable
and each contains in itself the whole world.
If you do not discriminate between coarse and fine
you will not be tempted to prejudice and opinion.

To live in the Great Way
is neither easy nor difficult,
but those with limited views
are fearful and irresolute:
the faster they hurry, the slower they go,
and clinging [attachment] cannot be limited:
even to be attached to the idea of enlightenment
is to go astray.
Just let things be in their own way

and there will be neither coming nor going.
Obey the nature of things [your own nature],
and you will walk freely and undisturbed.
When thought is in bondage the truth is hidden,
for everything is murky and unclear
and the burdensome practice of judging
brings annoyance and weariness.
What benefit can be derived
from distinctions and separations?

If you wish to move in the One Way
do not dislike even the world of senses and ideas.
Indeed, to accept them fully
is identical with true Enlightenment.
The wise man strives to no goals
but the foolish man fetters himself.
There is one Dharma, not many;
distinctions arise
from the clinging needs of the ignorant.
To seek Mind with the [discriminating] mind
is the greatest of all mistakes.

Rest and unrest derive from passion;
with enlightenment there is no liking and disliking.
All dualities come from ignorant inference.
They are like dreams or flowers in air:
foolish to try to grasp them.
Gain and loss, right and wrong:
such thoughts must finally be abolished at once.

If the eye never sleeps,
all dreams will naturally cease.

If the mind makes no discriminations,
the ten thousand things are as they are, of single
    essence.
To understand the mystery of this One essence
is to be released from all entanglements.
When all things are seen equally
the timeless Self-essence is reached.
No comparisons or analogies are possible
in this causeless, relationless state.

Consider movement stationary
and the stationary in motion,
both movement and rest disappear.
When such dualities cease to exist
Oneness itself cannot exist.
To this ultimate finality
no law or description applies.

For the unified mind in accord with the Way
All self-centered striving ceases.
Doubts and irresolutions vanish
and life in true faith is possible.
With a single stroke we are free from bondage;
nothing clings to us and we hold to nothing.
All is empty, clear, self-illuminating,
with no exertion of the mind's power.
Here thought, feeling, knowledge, and imagination
    are of no value.
In this world of Suchness
there is neither self nor other-than-self.
To come directly into harmony with this reality

just simply say when doubt arises, "Not two."
In this "not two" nothing is separate,
nothing is excluded.
No matter when or where,
enlightenment means entering this truth.
And this truth is beyond extension or diminution in
    time or space;
in it a single thought is ten thousand years.

Emptiness here, Emptiness there,
but the infinite universe stands
always before your eyes.
Infinitely large and infinitely small;
no difference, for definitions have vanished
and no boundaries are seen.
So too with Being and non-Being.
Don't waste time in doubts and arguments
that have nothing to do with this.

One thing, all things:
move among and intermingle,
without distinction.
To live in this realization
is to be without anxiety about non-perfection.
To live in this faith is the road to non-duality.
Because the non-dual is one with the trusting mind.

Words!
The Way is beyond language,
for in it there is
   no yesterday
   no tomorrow
   no today.

*translated by Richard B. Clarke*

# PRACTICE OF

# MEDITATION

## *by Zen Master Dogen*

TRUTH is perfect and complete in itself. It is not something newly discovered; it has always existed.

Truth is not far away; it is ever present. It is not something to be attained since not one of your steps leads away from it.

Do not follow the ideas of others, but learn to listen to the voice within yourself. Your body and mind will become clear and you will realize the unity of all things.

The slightest movement of your dualistic thought will prevent you from entering the palace of meditation and wisdom.

The Buddha meditated for six years, Bodhidharma for nine. The practice of meditation is not a method for the attainment of realization—it is enlightenment itself.

Your search among books, word upon word, may lead you to the depths of knowledge, but it is not the way to receive the reflection of your true self.

When you have thrown off your ideas as to mind and body, the original truth will fully appear. Zen is simply the expression of truth; therefore longing and striving are not the true attitudes of Zen.

To actualize the blessedness of meditation you should practice with pure intention and firm determination. Your meditation room should be clean and quiet. Do not dwell in thoughts of good or bad. Just relax and forget that you are meditating. Do not desire realization since that thought will keep you confused.

Sit on a cushion in a manner as comfortable as possible, wearing loose clothing. Hold your body straight without leaning to the left or the right, forward or backward. Your ears should be in line with your shoulders, and your nose in a straight line with your navel. Keep your tongue at the roof of your mouth and close your lips. Keep your eyes slightly open, and breathe through your nostrils.

Before you begin meditation take several slow, deep breaths. Hold your body erect, allowing your breathing to become normal again. Many thoughts will crowd into your mind, ignore them, letting them go. If they persist be aware of them with the awareness which does not think. In other words, think non-thinking.

Zen meditation is not physical culture, nor is it a method to gain something material. It is peacefulness and blessedness itself. It is the actualization of truth and wisdom.

In your meditation you yourself are the mirror reflecting the solution of your problems. The human mind has absolute freedom within its true nature. You can attain your freedom intuitively. Do not work for freedom, rather allow the practice itself to be liberation.

When you wish to rest, move your body slowly and stand up quietly. Practice this meditation in the morning or in the evening, or at any leisure time during the day. You will soon realize that your mental burdens are dropping away one by one, and that you are gaining an intuitive power hitherto unnoticed.

There are thousands upon thousands of students who have practiced meditation and obtained its fruits. Do not doubt its possibilities because of the simplicity of the method. If you cannot find the truth right where you are, where else do you expect to find it?

Life is short and no one knows what the next moment will bring. Open your mind while you have the opportunity, thereby gaining the treasures of wisdom, which in turn you can share abundantly with others, bringing them happiness.

*adapted from the* FUKANZAZENGI,
*translated by Senzaki and McCandless*

# ACTUALIZING THE FUNDAMENTAL POINT

*by Zen Master Dogen*

As all things are buddha-dharma, there is delusion and realization, practice, and birth and death, and there are buddhas and sentient beings.

As the myriad things are without an abiding self, there is no delusion, no realization, no buddha, no sentient being, no birth and death.

The buddha way is, basically, leaping clear of the many and the one; thus there are birth and death, delusion and realization, sentient beings and buddhas.

Yet in attachment blossoms fall, and in aversion weeds spread.

To carry yourself forward and experience myriad things is delusion. That myriad things come forth and experience themselves is awakening.

Those who have great realization of delusion are buddhas; those who are greatly deluded about realization are sentient beings. Further, there are those who continue realizing beyond realization, who are in delusion throughout delusion.

When buddhas are truly buddhas they do not necessarily notice that they are buddhas. However, they are actualized buddhas, who go on actualizing buddhas.

To study the buddha way is to study the self. To study the self is to forget the self. To forget the self is to be actualized by myriad things. When actualized by myriad things, your body and mind as well as the bodies and minds of others drop away. No trace of realization remains, and this no-trace continues endlessly.

When you ride in a boat and watch the shore, you might assume that the shore is moving. But when you keep your eyes closely on the boat, you can see that the boat moves. Similarly, if you examine myriad things with a confused body and mind you might suppose that your mind and nature are permanent. When you practice intimately and return to where you are, it will be clear that nothing at all has unchanging self.

Firewood becomes ash, and it does not become firewood again. Yet, do not suppose that the ash is future and the firewood past. You should understand that firewood is firewood, which fully includes past and future. Ash is ash, which fully includes future and past. Just as firewood does not become firewood again after it is ash, you do not return to birth after death.

This being so, it is an established way in buddha-dharma to deny that birth turns into death. Accordingly, birth is understood as no-birth. It is an unshakable teaching in Buddha's discourse that death does not turn into birth. Accordingly, death is understood as no-death.

Birth is an expression complete this moment. Death is an expression complete this moment. They are like winter and spring. You do not call winter the beginning of spring, nor summer the end of spring.

Enlightenment is like the moon reflected on the water. The moon does not get wet, nor is the water broken. Although its light is wide and great, the moon is reflected even in a puddle an inch wide. The whole moon and the entire sky are reflected in dewdrops on the grass, or even in one drop of water.

Enlightenment does not divide you, just as the moon does not break the water. You cannot hinder enlightenment, just as a drop of water does not hinder the moon in the sky.

The depth of the drop is the height of the moon. Each reflection, however long or short its duration, manifests the vastness of the dewdrop, and realizes the limitlessness of the moonlight in the sky.

When dharma does not fill your whole body and mind, you think it is already sufficient. When dharma fills your body and mind, you understand that something is missing.

For example, when you sail out in a boat to the middle of an ocean where no land is in sight, and view the four directions, the ocean looks circular, and does not look any other way. But the ocean is neither round nor square; its features are infinite in variety. It is like a palace. It is like a jewel. It only looks circular as far as you can see at that time. All things are like this.

Though there are many features in the dusty world and the world beyond conditions, you see and understand only what your eye of practice can reach. In order to learn the nature of the myriad things, you must know that although they may look round or square, the other features of oceans and mountains are infinite in variety; whole worlds are there. It is so not only around you, but also directly beneath your feet, or in a drop of water.

A fish swims in the ocean, and no matter how far it swims there is no end to the water. A bird flies in the sky, and no matter how far it flies there is no end to the air. However, the fish and the bird have never left their elements. When their activity is large their field is large. When their need is small their field is small. Thus, each of them totally covers its full range, and each of them totally experiences its realm. If the bird leaves the air it will die at once. If the fish leaves the water it will die at once.

Know that water is life and air is life. The bird is life and the fish is life. Life must be the bird and life must be the fish.

It is possible to illustrate this with more analogies. Practice, enlightenment, and people are like this.

Now if a bird or a fish tries to reach the end of its element before moving in it, this bird or this fish will not find its way or its place. When you find your place where you are, practice occurs, actualizing the fundamental point. When you find your way at this moment, practice occurs, actualizing the fundamental point; for the place, the way, is neither large nor small, neither yours nor others'. The place, the way, has not carried over from the past, and it is not merely arising now.

Accordingly, in the practice-enlightenment of the buddha way, meeting one thing is mastering it—doing one practice is practicing completely.

Zen master Baoche of Mt. Mayu was fanning himself. A monk approached and said, "Master, the nature of wind is permanent and there is no place it does not reach. Why, then, do you fan yourself?"

"Although you understand that the nature of the wind is permanent," Baoche replied, "you do not understand the meaning of its reaching everywhere."

"What is the meaning of its reaching everywhere?" asked the monk again. The master just kept fanning himself. The monk bowed deeply.

The actualization of the buddha-dharma, the vital path of its correct transmission, is like this. If you say that you do not need to fan yourself because the nature of wind is permanent and you can have wind without fanning, you will understand neither permanence nor the nature of wind. The nature of wind is permanent; because of that, the wind of the buddha's house brings forth the gold of the earth and makes fragrant the cream of the long river.

*adapted from the* GENJO KOAN,
*translated by Robert Aitken and Kazuaki Tanahashi*

# THE NATURAL ABIDING

*by the nun Niguma*

Don't do anything whatsoever with the mind—
Abide in an authentic, natural state.
One's own mind, unwavering, is reality.
The key is to meditate like this without wavering;
Experience the great reality beyond extremes.
In a pellucid ocean,
Bubbles arise and dissolve again.
Just so, thoughts are no different from ultimate reality,
So don't find fault; remain at ease.
Whatever arises, whatever occurs,
Don't grasp—release it on the spot.
Appearances, sounds, and objects are one's own mind;
There's nothing except mind.
Mind is beyond the extremes of birth and death.
The nature of mind, awareness,
Although using the objects of the five senses,
Does not wander from reality.
In the state of cosmic equilibrium
There is nothing to abandon or practice,
No meditation or post-meditation. Just this.

*translated by Miranda Shaw*

# ENLIGHTENMENT

# HAS NO FORM

ENLIGHTENMENT has no definite form or nature by which it can manifest itself; so in enlightenment itself, there is nothing to be enlightened. Enlightenment exists solely because of delusion and ignorance; if they disappear, so will Enlightenment. And the opposite is true also: there is no Enlightenment apart from delusion and ignorance; no delusion and ignorance apart from Enlightenment. Therefore be on guard against thinking of enlightenment as a "thing" to be grasped at, lest it, too, should become an obstruction. When the mind that was in darkness becomes enlightened, it passes away, and with its passing, the thing which we call Enlightenment passes also.

As long as people desire Enlightenment and grasp after it, it means that delusion is still with them; therefore, they who are following the way to Enlightenment must not grasp at it, and if they reach Enlightenment they must not linger in it. When people attain Enlightenment in this sense, it means that everything is Enlightenment itself as it is; therefore, people should follow the path to Enlightenment until in their thoughts, worldly passions and Enlightenment become identical as they are.

This concept of universal oneness—that things in their essential nature have no distinguishing marks—is called Emptiness. Emptiness means non-substantiality, the un-born, having no self-nature, no duality. It is because things in themselves have no form or characteristics that we can speak of them as neither being born nor being destroyed. There is nothing about the essential nature of things that can be described in terms of discrimination; that is why things are called nonsubstantial.

As has been pointed out, all things appear and disappear because of causes and conditions. Nothing ever exists entirely alone; everything is in relation to everything else. Wherever there is light, there is shadow; wherever there is length, there is shortness; wherever there is white, there is black. Just like these, as the self-nature of things cannot exist alone, they are called nonsubstantial.

By the same reasoning, Enlightenment cannot exist apart from ignorance, nor ignorance apart from Enlightenment. Since things do not differ in their essential nature, there can be no duality. It is a mistake for people to seek a thing supposed to be good and right and to flee from another supposed to be bad and evil.

If people insist that all things are empty and transitory, it is as great a mistake as to insist that things are real and do not change. If people become attached to a self, it is a mistake because it cannot save them from suffering. If they believe that there is no self, it is also a mistake and it would be useless for them to practice the Way of Truth. If people assert that everything is suffering, it is also a mistake; if they assert that everything is happiness, that is a mistake, too. All duality merges in the Middle Way.

*adapted from the* LANKAVATARA SUTRA,
*translated by Bukkyo Dendo Kyokai*

# SONG OF MAHAMUDRA

### *by Tilopa*

MAHAMUDRA* is beyond all words and symbols,
But for you, Naropa, earnest and loyal, must this
be said.

The Void needs no reliance; Mahamudra rests on
   naught.
Without making an effort, but remaining natural,
One can break the yoke thus gaining liberation.

If one looks for naught when staring into space;
If with the mind one then observes the mind;
One destroys distinctions and reaches Buddhahood.

The clouds that wander through the sky have no
   roots, no home,
Nor do the distinctive thoughts floating through the
   mind.
Once the Self-mind is seen, Discrimination stops.

In space, shapes and colors form
But neither by black nor white is space tinged.

---

*Mahamudra is the practice and teaching that leads to the
realization of One Mind.

From the Self-mind all things emerge;
The Mind by virtues and by vices is not stained.

The darkness of ages cannot shroud the glowing sun;
The long eons of Samsara ne'er can hide the Mind's
    brilliant Light.

Though words are spoken to explain the Void, the
    Void as such can never be expressed. Though we
    say "the Mind is a bright light," it is beyond all
    words and symbols. Although the Mind is void in
    essence, all things it embraces and contains.

Do naught with the body but relax;
Shut firm the mouth and silent remain;
Empty your mind and think of naught.
Like a hollow bamboo rest at ease your body.
Giving not nor taking, put your mind at rest.
Mahamudra is like a mind that clings to naught.
Thus practicing, in time you will reach Buddhahood.
The practice of Mantra and Perfections, instruction
    in the Sutras and Precepts, and teaching from the
    Schools and Scriptures will not bring realization
    of the Innate Truth.
For if the mind when filled with some desire should
    seek a goal, it only hides the Light.

One who keeps Tantric Precepts yet discriminates,
    betrays the vows of Awakening,
Cease all activity; abandon all desire; let thoughts rise
    and fall as they will like the ocean waves.

One who never harms the Non-abiding nor the
   Principles of non-distinction, upholds the
   Tantric Precepts.
He who abandons craving and clings not to this or
   that,
Perceives the real meaning given in the Scriptures.

In Mahamudra all one's sins are burned; in
   Mahamudra one is released from the prison of
   this world. This is the Dharma's supreme torch.
   Those who disbelieve it are fools who ever wallow
   in misery and sorrow.

To strive for Liberation one should rely on a Guru.
   When your mind receives the Guru's blessing
   emancipation is at hand.

Alas, all things in this world are meaningless; they are
   but sorrow's seeds. Small teachings lead to acts.
   One should only follow teachings that are great.

To transcend duality is the Kingly View; to conquer
   distractions is the Royal Practice; the Path of
   No-practice is the Way of Buddhas. One who
   treads that Path reaches Buddhahood.

Transient is this world; like phantoms and dreams,
Substance it has none. Grasp not the world nor your
   kin;
Cut the strings of lust and hatred; meditate in woods
   and mountains.

If without effort you remain loosely in the "natural
state," soon Mahamudra you will win and attain
the Non-attainment.

Cut the root of a tree and the leaves will wither;
Cut the root of your mind and Samsara falls.

The light of any lamp dispels in a moment the
darkness of long eons;
The strong light of the mind in but a flash will burn
the veil of ignorance.

Whoever clings to mind sees not the truth of what's
beyond the mind.
Whoever strives to practice Dharma finds not the
truth of Beyond-practice.
One should cut cleanly through the root of mind
and stare naked.
One should thus break away from all distinctions
and remain at ease.

One should not give or take but remain natural,
for Mahamudra is beyond all acceptance and
rejection.
Since the consciousness is not born, no one can
obstruct or soil it;
Staying in the "Unborn" realm all appearances will
dissolve into the ultimate Dharma.
All self-will and pride will vanish into naught.

The supreme Understanding transcends all this and
that.

The supreme Action embraces great resourcefulness
    without attachment.
The supreme Accomplishment is to realize
    immanence without hope.

At first a yogi feels the mind is tumbling like a
    waterfall;
In mid-course, like the Ganges, it flows on slow
    and gentle;
In the end, it is a great vast ocean,
Where the Lights of Child and Mother merge in one.

*adapted from the translation by Garma C. C. Chang*

# DEVELOPMENT

# OF MAHAMUDRA

Iₙ these twenty-one practices, you will initially develop the state of calm which is the root of all meditation, and you will learn to contemplate one-pointedly. You will first use external objects (such as an ordinary pebble or twig, or a holy image of the Buddha) to meditate upon and only then begin to meditate without using any external objects at all. Following this, subsequent practices will lead you to examine the nature of mind and to the realization of Mahamudra.

Develop these practices one by one.

PRACTICE 1: Focusing upon an ordinary pebble or twig. For this session, set out a small pebble in front of you as your meditative object; and just stare at it one-pointedly, letting your awareness neither stray from it nor identify with it.

PRACTICE 2: Focusing upon an image of the Buddha. Here you may concentrate upon an image to symbolize the body of the Buddha, a syllable to symbolize his speech, or a glowing dot to symbolize his mind.

PRACTICE 3: In this practice, you will focus upon a syllable; so visualize in front of you the disc of a moon, the size of a fingernail, and upon it the syllable HUM, as fine as if it were written with a single hair, and concentrate upon this.

PRACTICE 4: Now you should focus upon a glowing dot visualized in front of you, in the shape of an egg and about the size of a pea, shining and wondrous, and concentrate upon this as before.

PRACTICE 5: Focusing upon the moving breath. Let your body and your mind be tranquil, and focus upon the inhalation and exhalation of your breath; and with no other thoughts simply count your breaths as they move in and out.

PRACTICE 6: In this practice, you will follow your breath as it is inhaled and exhaled; and note for how long the breath is exhaled, and for how long it is inhaled, and through how much of your body it moves.

PRACTICE 7: Now let your awareness move with your breath, from the tip of your nose all the way down to your navel, and watch how it goes and comes and is held within.

PRACTICE 8: Now spend the sessions examining individually the five elements of earth, air, fire, water, and space which make up your body, and you will become aware of how the breath increases and decreases as it moves in and out.

PRACTICE 9: And finally sense the air to be white as

it is exhaled, blue as it is inhaled, and red as it is held within, and the motion of the breath will become visible to you.

PRACTICE 10: Holding the breath. Breathe out forcibly three times, then gently draw in the upper air through your nose and draw up the lower air from your intestines, and try to hold it as long as you can until your thoughts are stopped and your mind no longer strays to external objects.

PRACTICE 11: Cutting off every thought that occurs, in the next session you will begin to meditate without using any external objects at all.

Continue to contemplate as in the previous practice; you will find your mind following after external objects, imposing its constructs upon them, and thinking that things are real. Do not let this continue, but discipline yourself with mindfulness, and try to prevent every single one of these thoughts. And thus contemplate, cutting off at its very root any thought that occurs.

PRACTICE 12: During these sessions, you will be able to contemplate like this for an ever increasing period of time; indeed, it will seem that these thoughts are becoming more numerous than before, and following one after the other as if in a continuous stream.

This is what we call recognizing your thoughts as you might become aware of an enemy; it is what we call the first state of calm, like the rushing of a mountain cataract.

PRACTICE 13: In this practice, you will now let these thoughts do whatever they want, not cutting them off at all, yet not falling under their spell.

PRACTICE 14: You now enter the middle state of calm, like the gentle flowing of a river. Now your thoughts can no longer move you one way or the other, and you can begin to abide one-pointedly in a state of calm.

To remain in this state continuously settles all the sediment in your mind. As Gampopa says: If you do not stir the water, it is clear; and if you leave your mind alone, it is blissful.

PRACTICE 15: Leaving your mind alone. In this practice you will keep your mind as if you were spinning a thread, keeping an even tension upon it. For if your contemplation is too tight, then it snaps; and if it is too loose, then you slip into indolence.

PRACTICE 16: Now in these sessions, you will keep your mind as if it were a snapped rope.

For all our prior antidotes to thoughts have been thoughts themselves; it is a thought to think that you must impose no constructs upon reality. You have simply substituted one thought for another: this is what we call mindfulness chasing an object, and it is a fault in contemplation.

So cast aside your mindfulness itself: keep your mind free of all effort and let it flow naturally and spontaneously in the stream of calm; this is what we call keeping your mind as if it were a snapped rope.

PRACTICE 17: Now you will try to keep your mind as if it were a child looking at the murals painted on a temple wall. For you are now without thought and without feeling in your body and mind: and thus you will see visions of smoke and other forms of emptiness: you may feel you are fainting, or as if floating in empty space.

When these ecstatic visions occur, you must neither enjoy them nor fear them and thus neither think they are important nor cling to them: this is what we call keeping your mind as if it were a child looking at the paintings in a temple.

PRACTICE 18: And finally you will keep your mind as if it were an elephant being pricked by a pin.

For while your mind is fixed, your mindfulness is automatically recognizing every thought that occurs. What is to be cast aside and that which casts aside meet each other, and your thoughts can no longer jump about from one to the next. The antidote to thought now occurs spontaneously and naturally, without needing any effort at all on your part: this is what we call mindfulness holding its object.

Thus you feel your thoughts occur, but you yourself never cut them off nor react to them in any way: this is what we call trying to prick an elephant with a pin.

And this is what we call the final state of calm, like an ocean without waves. You recognize the changing within the changeless, and you simply leave it alone, for you see the changeless within the changing.

PRACTICE 19: In these sessions, you will now analyze this changeless and changing, to gain the realization of insight, and you may finally reach the state of meditationless meditation.

Enter the state of calm wherein you are no longer imposing any constructs upon reality, but simply letting it appear before you. Look upon your changelessness and see its true nature; see how it is changeless and see how it changes from its state of changelessness.

Are the changes in the mind something other than the changeless, or is it a changing within the changeless itself? What is the true nature of this changing? And how does the changing stop?

PRACTICE 20: And now you are beginning to realize that you cannot see the changeless apart from the changing, or the changing apart from the changeless; you cannot find the true nature of the changeless or the changing.

You are beginning to see that your introspection is finding nothing there at all, that the watched and the watcher are both the same. You cannot set out its true nature: it is what we call the vision beyond all thought.

PRACTICE 21: The realization of final insight. Now you know how to leave every thought and passion entirely alone, not cutting it off at all yet not falling under its spell.

During these sessions, try simply to recognize every thought for what it is: let it spontaneously become emptiness, pure in and of itself, without your casting it aside. In this way you learn how to make use of all hindrances; this is what we call making a hindrance into the path itself.

By just recognizing the thought, the imposition of a construct, you are freed from it spontaneously; you realize that there is no difference at all between what you cast aside and that which casts aside.

And now too there is born in you exceeding compassion for all those living creatures who do not realize the essence of their minds. And you will spend your lives working for the sake of these others, but all your meditations have now cleansed away any idea that these others really exist.

And it is with regard to practice such as this that we say: I neither keep nor cast aside anything that happens on the path.

CONCLUSION: Meditationless meditation. And now you have realized that every event is innate and spontaneous and is the body of reality itself, as the world appears before you in your meditationless meditation. For the passions are finished, the antidote which casts them aside is finished; and the circle is broken. There is no place else to go; the journey is over; there is no place higher than this.

As it is said: Ha! This is the knowledge of my own experience. It is beyond the ways of speech; it is not an object of the mind. I have nothing to teach at all: know

# TIBETAN BOOK OF THE

# GREAT LIBERATION

THERE being really no duality, separation is untrue. Until duality is transcended and at-one-ment realized, Enlightenment cannot be attained. The whole Samsara and Nirvana, as an inseparable unity, are one's mind.

Owing to worldly beliefs, which one is free to accept or reject, a person wanders in Samsara. Therefore, practicing the Dharma, freed from every attachment, grasp the whole essence of these teachings.

Although the One Mind is, it has not existence.

When one seeks one's mind in its true state, it is found to be quite intelligible, although invisible. In its true state, mind is naked, immaculate; not made of anything, being of the Voidness; clear, vacuous, without duality, transparent, timeless, uncompounded, unimpeded, colorless; not realizable as a separate thing, but as the unity of all things, yet not composed of them; of one taste, and transcendent over differentiation.

The One Mind being verily of the Voidness and without any foundation, one's mind is likewise as vacuous as the sky. To know whether this is so or not, look within thine own mind. Being merely a flux of instability like the air of the firmament, objective appearances are without power to fascinate and fetter. To know whether this be so or not, look within thine own mind. Arising of themselves and being naturally free like the clouds in the sky, all external appearances verily fade away into their own respective places. To know whether this be so or not, look within thine own mind. The Dharma being nowhere save in the mind, there is no other place of meditation than the mind. The Dharma being nowhere save in the mind, there is no other doctrine to be taught or practiced elsewhere. The Dharma being nowhere save in the mind, there is no other place of truth for the observance of a vow. The Dharma being nowhere save in the mind, there is no Dharma elsewhere whereby Liberation may be attained. Again and again look within thine own mind.

When looking outward into the vacuity of space, there is no place to be found where the mind is shining. When looking inward into one's own mind in search of the shining, there is to be found no thing that shines.

One's own mind is transparent, without quality. Being void of quality it is comparable to a cloudless sky.

The state of mind transcendent over all dualities brings Liberation.

Again and again, look within thine own mind.

*translated by W. Y. Evans-Wentz*

# TIBETAN BOOK

# OF THE DEAD

Remember the clear light, the pure clear white light from which everything in the universe comes, to which everything in the universe returns; the original nature of your own mind. The natural state of the universe unmanifest.

Let go into the clear light, trust it, merge with it. It is your own true nature, it is home.

The visions you experience exist within your consciousness; the forms they take are determined by your past attachments, your past desires, your past fears, your past karma.

These visions have no reality outside your consciousness. No matter how frightening some of them may seem they cannot hurt you. Just let them pass through your consciousness. They will all pass in time. No need to become involved with them; no need to become attracted to the beautiful visions; no need to be repulsed by the frightening ones. No need to be seduced or excited by the sexual ones. No need to be attached to them at all.

Just let them pass. If you become involved with

these visions, you may wander for a long time confused. Just let them pass through your consciousness like clouds passing through an empty sky.

Fundamentally they have no more reality than this.

Remember these teachings, remember the clear light, the pure bright shining white light of your own nature, it is deathless.

If you can look into the visions you can experience and recognize that they are composed of the same pure clear white light as everything else in the universe.

No matter where or how far you wander, the light is only a split second, a half-breath away. It is never too late to recognize the clear light.

*adapted from the translation by W. Y. Evans-Wentz*

# FINDING THE WAY

"Followers of the Way, the one right here before your eyes and listening to the Dharma is the person who 'enters fire without being burned, goes into water without being drowned, and plays about in the three deepest hells as if in a fairground; that person enters the world of hungry spirits and dumb animals without being molested by them.'

"Why is this so? Because there is nothing that person dislikes. If you love the sacred and dislike the worldly, you will go on floating and sinking in the ocean of birth and death. The passions arise depending on the heart. If the heart is stilled, where then do you seize the passions? Do not tire yourselves by making up discriminations; and quite naturally, of itself, you will find the Way."

*from* RINZAI ROKU,
*translated by Irmgard Schloegl*

# NOT MIXING

# UP BUDDHISM

Once a monk on pilgrimage met a woman living in a hut. The monk asked, "Do you have any disciples?"

The woman said, "Yes."

The monk said, "Where are they?"

She said, "The mountains, rivers and earth, the plants and trees, are all my disciples."

The monk said, "Are you a nun?"

She said, "What do you see me as?"

He said, "A layperson."

The woman in the hut said, "You can't be a monk!"

The monk said, "You shouldn't mix up Buddhism."

She said, "I'm not mixing up Buddhism."

The monk said, "Aren't you mixing up Buddhism this way?"

She said, "You're a man, I'm a woman—where has there ever been any mixup?"

*translated by Thomas Cleary*

# THE BODHISATTVA

"THE Bodhisattva comes as neither coming nor going; the Bodhisattva comes as neither moving nor staying, as neither dead nor born, as neither staying nor passing away, as neither departing nor rising, as neither hoping nor getting attached, as neither doing nor reaping the reward, as neither being born nor gone to annihilation, as neither eternal nor bound for death.

"And yet it is in this way that the Bodhisattva comes: he comes where an all-embracing love abides, because he desires to discipline all beings; he comes where there is a great compassionate heart, because he desires to protect all beings against suffering; he comes where there are deeds of morality, because he desires to be born wherever he can be agreeable; he comes wherever there are great vows to fulfill because of the power of the original vows; he comes out of the miraculous powers because wherever he is sought after he manifests himself to please people; he comes where there is effortlessness because he is never away from the footsteps of all the Buddhas; he comes where there is neither giving nor taking because in his movements mental and physical there is no trace of striving; he comes out of the skillful means born of transcendental knowledge because he is ever in conformity with the mentalities of all beings; he comes where transformations are manifested because all that appears is like a reflection, like a transformed body."

*from* THE FLOWER ORNAMENT SUTRA,

*translated by D. T. Suzuki*

# BODHICHITTA

*The Heartfelt Wish for Awakening*

THE Bodhichitta is like a seed because from it grows all the truths of Buddhism. It is like a farm because here are produced all things of purity for the world.

The Bodhichitta is like the earth because all the worlds are supported by it. It is like water because all the dirt of the passions is thereby cleansed. It is like the wind because it blows all over the world with nothing obstructing its course. It is like fire because it consumes all the fuel of bad logic.

The Bodhichitta is like the sun because it leaves nothing unenlightened on earth. It is like the moon because it fills to perfection all things of purity. It is like a lamp because it perceives where the road is even and where it is uneven.

The Bodhichitta is like a highway because it leads one to the city of knowledge. It is like a sacred ford because it keeps away all that is not proper. It is like a carriage because it carries all the Bodhisattvas. It is like a door because it opens to all the doings of the Bodhisattva.

The Bodhichitta is like a mansion because it is the retreat where Samādhi and meditation are practised. It is like a park because it is where the enjoyment of truth is experienced. It is like a dwelling-house because it is where all the world is comfortably sheltered. It is like a refuge because it gives a salutary abode to all beings. It is like an asylum because it is where all the Bodhisattvas walk.

The Bodhichitta is like a father because it protects all the Bodhisattvas. It is like a mother because it brings up all the Bodhisattvas. It is like a nurse because it takes care of all the Bodhisattvas. It is like a good friend because it gives good advice to all the Bodhisattvas. It is like a king because it overpowers the minds of all the Shravakas and the Pratyekabuddhas. It is like a great sovereign because it fulfils all the excellent vows.

The Bodhichitta is like a great ocean because it harbours all the gems of virtues. It is like Mount Sumeru because it towers impartially above all things. It is like Mount Cakravada because it supports all the world. It is like Mount Himalaya because it produces all sorts of knowledge-herbs. It is like Mount Gandhamadana because it harbours all kinds of virtue-fragrance. It is like space because it infinitely spreads out the merit of goodness.

*from the* GANDAVYUHA SUTRA,
*translated by D. T. Suzuki*

# DIAMOND SUTRA

"Subhuti, someone who has set out in the vehicle of a Bodhisattva should produce a thought in this manner: 'As many beings as there are in the universe of beings, comprehended under the term *beings*—either egg-born, or born from a womb, or moisture-born, or miraculously born; with or without form; with perception, without perception, or with neither perception nor non-perception—as far as any conceivable universe of beings is concerned: all these should by me be led to Nirvana, into that Realm of Nirvana which leaves nothing behind. And yet, although innumerable beings have thus been led to Nirvana, no being at all has been led to Nirvana.' And why? If in a Bodhisattva the perception of a 'being' should take place, he could not be called a 'Bodhi-being.' And why? He is not to be called a Bodhi-being in whom the perception of a self or a being would take place, or the perception of a living soul or a person."

*translated by Edward Conze*

# PERFECTION OF GIVING

SARIPUTRA: "What is the worldly, and what is the supramundane perfection of giving?"

Subhuti: "The worldly perfection of giving consists in this: The Bodhisattva gives liberally to all those who ask, all the while thinking in terms of real things. It occurs to him: 'I give, that one receives, this is the gift. I renounce all my possessions without stint. I act as one who knows the Buddha. I practice the perfection of giving. I, having made this gift into the common property of all beings, dedicate it to supreme enlightenment, and that without apprehending anything. By means of this gift and its fruit may all beings in this very life be at their ease, and may they one day enter Nirvana!' Tied by three ties he gives a gift. Which three? A perception of self, a perception of others, a perception of the gift.

"The supramundane perfection of giving, on the other hand, consists in the threefold purity. What is the threefold purity? Here a Bodhisattva gives a gift, and he does not apprehend a self, nor a recipient, nor a gift; also no reward of his giving. He surrenders that gift to all beings, but he apprehends neither beings nor self. He dedicates that gift to supreme enlightenment, but he does not apprehend any enlightenment. This is called the supramundane perfection of giving."

*from* THE PERFECTION OF WISDOM IN
25,000 LINES, *translated by Edward Conze*

# SUTRA OF HUI-NENG

"Now that you have already taken refuge in the threefold body of Buddha, I shall expound to you the four great vows. Good friends, recite in unison what I say: 'I vow to save all sentient beings everywhere. I vow to cut off all the passions everywhere. I vow to study all the Buddhist teachings everywhere. I vow to achieve the unsurpassed Buddha Way.'

"Learned Audience, all of us have now declared that we vow to deliver an infinite number of sentient beings; but what does this mean? It does not mean that I, Hui-neng, am going to deliver them. And who are these sentient beings within our mind? They are the delusive mind, the deceitful mind, the evil mind, and suchlike minds—all these are sentient beings. Each of them has to deliver itself by means of its own essence of mind. Then the deliverance is genuine.

"Now, what does it mean to deliver oneself by one's own essence of mind? It means the deliverance of the ignorant, the elusive, and the vexatious beings within our mind by means of right views.

"Enlightened by right views, we call forth the buddha within us.

When our nature is dominated by the three poisonous
    elements
We are said to be possessed by Mara;
But when right views eliminate from our mind these
    poisonous elements
Mara will be transformed into a real buddha.

"When our temperament is such that we are no longer
    the slaves of the five sense objects,
And when we have realized the essence of mind even
    for one moment only, then truth is known to us.

"One who is able to realize the truth within one's own
    mind
Has sown the seed of buddhahood.

"Hear me, future disciples!
Your time will have been badly wasted if you neglect to
    put this teaching into practice."

"What you should do is to know your own mind
and realize your own buddha-nature, which neither
rests nor moves, neither becomes nor ceases to be, neither comes nor goes, neither affirms nor denies, neither stays nor departs.

"Imperturbable and serene, the ideal person practices
    no virtue.
Self-possessed and dispassionate, no sin is committed.
Calm and silent, seeing and hearing are given up.
Even and upright, the mind abides nowhere."

*adapted from the translations by*
*Philip Yampolsky and A. F. Price*

# HYAKUJO AND THE FOX

*The Koan*

When abbot Hyakujo gave a lecture on Zen, an old man sat listening with the monks and always left when they did. One day, however, he stayed behind, and Hyakujo asked him, "Who are you, standing here before me?" The old man answered, "I am not a human being. In the distant past, I was the head of this monastery. Once a monk asked me, 'Does an enlightened person fall under the law of karma or not?' I replied, 'Such a person does not fall under the law of karma.' Because of this answer, I was reborn as a fox for five hundred lives. Please tell me the turning words that will release me from this fox body."

Then he asked Hyakujo, "Does an enlightened person fall under the law of karma?"

Hyakujo replied, "Such a person does not ignore karma."

Hearing this, the old man was immediately enlightened and bowing to Hyakujo said, "I have now been released from the fox body."

*Mumon's Comment*

Not falling under the law of Karma." Why did he fall into the life of a fox? "Not ignoring karma." Why was he released from the fox body? If you have the eyes to understand all this, then you will know how the former abbot lived five hundred happy years as a fox.

*from the* MUMONKAN,
*translated by Gil Fronsdal*

# BETWEEN BIRTH
# AND DEATH

THOSE who are afraid of the sorrow which arises from the round of birth-and-death seek for Nirvana; they do not realize that between birth-and-death and Nirvana there is really no difference at all. They see Nirvana as the absence of all becoming, and the cessation of all contact of sense-organ and sense-object, and they will not understand that it is really only the inner realization of the store of impressions. Hence they teach the three Vehicles, but not the doctrine that nothing truly exists but the mind, in which are no images. Therefore, they do not know the extent of what has been perceived by the minds of past, present, and future Buddhas, and continue in the conviction that the world extends beyond the range of the mind's eye. And so they keep on rolling on the wheel of birth-and-death.

*from the* LANKAVATARA SUTRA,
*translated by* A. L. Basham

# BIRTH AND DEATH

# ARE NIRVANA

*by Zen Master Dogen*

JUST understand that birth and death itself is nirvana, and you will neither hate one as being birth and death nor cherish the other as being nirvana. Only then can you be free of birth and death.

This present birth and death is the life of Buddha. If you reject it with distaste, you are thereby losing the life of Buddha. If you abide in it, attaching to birth and death, you also lose the life of Buddha. But do not try to gauge it with your mind or speak it with words. When you simply release and forget both your body and your mind and throw yourself into the house of Buddha, then with no strength needed and no thought expended, freed from birth and death, you become Buddha. Then there can be no obstacle in any person's mind.

There is an extremely easy way to become Buddha. Refraining from all evil, not clinging to birth and death, working in deep compassion for all sentient beings, respecting those over you and having pity for those below you, without any detesting or desiring, worrying or lamentation—this is what is called Buddha. Do not search beyond it.

*translated by Masao Abe and Norman Waddell*

# TEACHINGS OF
# HUANG PO

"Your true nature is something never lost to you even in moments of delusion, nor is it gained at the moment of Enlightenment. It is the Nature of the Suchness. In it is neither delusion nor right understanding. It fills the Void everywhere and is intrinsically of the substance of the One Mind. How, then, can your mind-created objects exist outside the Void? The Void is fundamentally without spacial dimensions, passions, activities, delusions or right understanding. You must clearly understand that in it there are no things, no men and no Buddhas; for this Void contains not the smallest hairbreadth of anything that can be viewed spacially; it depends on nothing and is attached to nothing. It is all-pervading, spotless beauty; it is the self-existent and uncreated Absolute. Then how can it even be a matter for discussion that the *real* Buddha has no mouth and preaches no Dharma, or that *real* hearing requires no ears, for who could hear it? Ah, it is a jewel beyond all price.

"This pure Mind, the source of everything, shines

forever and on all with the brilliance of its own perfection. But the people of the world do not awake to it, regarding only that which sees, hears, feels and knows as mind. Blinded by their own sight, hearing, feeling and knowing, they do not perceive the spiritual brilliance of the source-substance. If they would only eliminate all conceptual thought in a flash, that source-substance would manifest itself like the sun ascending through the void and illuminating the whole universe without hindrance or bounds. Therefore, if you students of the Way seek to progress through seeing, hearing, feeling and knowing, when you are deprived of your perceptions, your way to Mind will be cut off and you will find nowhere to enter. Only realize that, though real Mind is expressed in these perceptions, it neither forms part of them nor is separate from them. You should not start *reasoning* from these perceptions, nor allow them to give rise to conceptual thought; yet nor should you seek the One Mind apart from them or abandon them in your pursuit of the Dharma. Do not keep them nor abandon them nor dwell in them nor cleave to them. Above, below, and around you, all is spontaneously existing, for there is nowhere which is outside the Buddha-Mind."

*from* THE ZEN TEACHING OF HUANG PO,
*translated by John Blofeld*

# MIND IS BUDDHA

*The Koan*

Taibai once asked Baso, "What is Buddha?"
Baso answered, "Mind is Buddha."

*Mumon's Poem*

A fine day under the blue sky!
Don't foolishly look here and there.
If you still ask, "What is Buddha?"
It is like pleading your innocence while clutching
stolen goods.

*from the* MUMONKAN,
*translated by Sumiko Kudo*

# ORDINARY MIND

# IS THE WAY

## The Koan

Joshu once asked Nansen, "What is the Way?" Nansen answered, "Ordinary mind is the Way." "Then should we direct ourselves toward it or not?" asked Joshu. "If you direct yourself toward it, you go away from it," answered Nansen. Joshu continued, "If we do not try, how can we know that it is the Way?" Nansen replied, "The Way does not belong to knowing or not-knowing. Knowing is illusion; not-knowing is blankness. If you really attain to the Way of no-doubt, it is like the great void, so vast and boundless. How, then, can there be right and wrong in the Tao?" At these words, Joshu was suddenly enlightened.

## Mumon's Poem

Hundreds of flowers in spring, the moon in autumn,
A cool breeze in summer, and snow in winter;
if there is no vain cloud in your mind
For you it is a good season.

*from the* MUMONKAN, *translated by Sumiko Kudo*

# PARABLE OF
# THE HIDDEN JEWEL

"WORLD-HONORED One! It is as if some man goes to an intimate friend's house, gets drunk, and falls asleep. Meanwhile his friend, having to go forth on official duty, ties a priceless jewel within his garment as a present, and departs. The man, being drunk and asleep, knows nothing of it. On arising he travels onward till he reaches some other country, where for food and clothing he expends much labor and effort, and undergoes exceedingly great hardship, and is content even if he can obtain but little. Later, his friend happens to meet him and speaks thus: 'Tut! Sir, how is it you have come to this for the sake of food and clothing? Wishing you to be in comfort and able to satisfy all your five senses, I formerly in such a year and month and on such a day tied a priceless jewel within your garment. Now as of old it is present there and you in ignorance are slaving and worrying to keep yourself alive. How little you have understood! Go you now and exchange that jewel for what you need and do whatever you will, free from all poverty and shortage.'"

*adapted from the* LOTUS SUTRA,
*translated by Bunno Kato and W. E. Soothill*

# SONG OF ZAZEN

*by Hakuin Zenji*

All beings by nature are Buddha,
as ice by nature is water.
Apart from water there is no ice;
apart from beings, no Buddha.

How sad that people ignore the near
and search for truth afar:
like someone in the midst of water
crying out in thirst;
like a child of a wealthy home
wandering among the poor.

Lost on dark paths of ignorance,
we wander through the Six Worlds;
from dark path to dark path—
when shall we be freed from birth and death?

Oh, the Zen meditation of the Mahayana!
To this the highest praise!
Devotion, repentance, training,
the many perfections—
all have their source in Zen meditation.

Those who try Zen meditation even once
wipe away beginningless crimes.
Where are all the dark paths then?
The Pure Land itself is near.

Those who hear this truth even once
and listen with a grateful heart,
treasuring it, revering it,
gain blessings without end.

Much more, those who turn about
and bear witness to self-nature,
self-nature that is no-nature,
go far beyond mere doctrine.

Here effect and cause are the same;
the Way is neither two nor three.
With form that is no-form,
going and coming, we are never astray;
with thought that is no-thought,
even singing and dancing are the voice of the Law.

How boundless and free is the sky of Awareness!
How bright the full moon of wisdom!
Truly, is anything missing now?
Nirvana is right here, before our eyes;
this very place is the Lotus Land;
this very body, the Buddha.

*adapted from the translation by Robert Aitken*

# SOURCES

*Agamas,* pp. 106–107: from E. Burneuf and P. Carus (trans.), *The Gospel of Buddha,* edited by Paul Carus (Chicago: Open Court, 1915).

*Anguttara Nikaya,* pp. 27, 48–51, 75–76: from Nyanaponika Thera (trans.), *Anguttara Nikaya: Discourses of the Buddha, an Anthology* (Kandy, Sri Lanka: Buddhist Publication Society, 1975).

*Anguttara Nikaya,* pp. 38, 102–103: from Nyanatiloka (trans.), *The Word of the Buddha* (Kandy, Ceylon: Buddhist Publication Society, 1971).

*Anguttara Nikaya,* pp. 93–95: from Andy Olendzki (trans.), *Inquiring Mind.*

*Anguttara Nikaya,* p. 121: from Kerry Brown and Joanne O'Brien (eds.), *The Essential Teachings of Buddhism* (London: Rider Books, 1989).

*Arousing the Supreme Mind,* p. 146: from Francis Cook (trans.), *How to Raise an Ox* (Los Angeles: Center Publications, 1978).

*Bhaddekaratta Sutta,* pp. 116–117: from Thich Nhat Hanh, *Our Appointment with Life* (Berkeley, Calif.: Parallax Press, 1990).

*Birth and Death Are Nirvana,* p. 197–198: from "Birth and Death," translated by Masao Abe and Norman Waddell, in *The Eastern Buddhist,* vol. 5, no. 1 (May, 1972).

*Bodhicharyavatara*, p. 132: from Eknath Easwaran, *God Makes the Rivers to Flow* (Tomales, Calif.: Nilgiri Press, n.d.).

*Buddhacarita*, p. 125: from *The Gospel of Buddha,* edited by Paul Carus (Chicago: Open Court, 1915).

*Buddhist Parables*, pp. 35–37: from E. W. Burlingame (trans.), *Buddhist Parables* (New Haven, Conn.: Yale University Press, 1922).

*Cullavagga*, p. 131: from T. W. Rhys-Davids (trans.), *The Gospel of Buddha,* edited by Paul Carus (Chicago: Open Court, 1915).

*Dhammapada*, pp. 1, 4, 8, 9, 14, 15, 21, 34, 44, 47, 54, 65, 85: from Thomas Byrom (trans.), *The Dhammapada: The Sayings of the Buddha* (New York: Alfred A. Knopf, 1976).

*Dhammapada*, pp. 24–25: from Nyanamoli Thera (ed.), *The Life of the Buddha* (Kandy, Sri Lanka: Buddhist Publication Society, 1978).

*Dhammapada Atthakatha*, p. 96: from Bukkyo Dendo Kyokai (trans.), *The Teachings of Buddha* (Tokyo: Bukkyo Dendo Kyokai, 1984).

*Diamond Sutra*, p. 145: from A. F. Price and Wong Mou-lam (trans.), *The Diamond Sutra and the Sutra of Hui-neng* (Boston: Shambhala Publications, 1990).

*Diamond Sutra*, p. 189: from Edward Conze (trans.), *Buddhist Wisdom Books* (London: George Allen & Unwin, 1958).

*Digha Nikaya*, pp. 7, 109: from Maurice Walshe (trans.), *Thus Have I Heard* (Boston: Wisdom Publications, 1987).

*Digha Nikaya*, pp. 80–81: from Bhikkhu Bodhi (trans.), *The Discourse on the Fruits of Recluseship* (Kandy, Sri Lanka: Buddhist Publication Society, 1989).

*Digha Nikaya*, p. 97: from Geoffrey Parrinder (ed.), *The Wisdom of the Early Buddhists* (New York: New Directions Publishing Corp., 1977).

## Sources

*The Flower Ornament Sutra,* pp. 185–186: from Sangh-arakshita, *The Eternal Legacy* (London: Therpa Publications, 1985).

*Fukanzazengi,* pp. 154–156: from Nyogen Senzaki and Ruth Strout McCandless, *Buddhism and Zen* (Berkeley, Calif.: North Point Press, 1987).

*Gandavyuha Sutra,* pp. 187–188: from D. T. Suzuki (trans.), *Essays in Zen Buddhism,* 3rd series (London: Rider and Co., 1953).

*Genjo Koan,* pp. 157–161: from Kazuaki Tanahashi (ed.), *Moon in a Dewdrop* (Berkeley, Calif.: North Point Press, 1986).

*The Gospel of the Buddha,* pp. 86–87, 98–99: from Paul Carus, *The Gospel of the Buddha* (Chicago: Open Court, 1915).

*Itivuttaka,* p. 105: from Sangharakshita, *The Eternal Legacy* (London: Therpa Publications, 1985).

*Khuddhaka Patha,* p. 108: from William de Bary (ed.), *The Buddhist Tradition* (New York: Vintage Books, 1972).

*Lalitavistara,* p. 133–134: from William de Bary (ed.), *The Buddhist Tradition* (New York: Vintage Books, 1972).

*Lankavatara Sutra,* p. 140: from D. T. Suzuki (trans.), *The Lankavatara Sutra* (London: Routledge & Kegan Paul, 1932).

*Lankavatara Sutra,* pp. 163–165: from Bukkyo Dendo Kyokai (trans.), *The Teachings of Buddha* (Tokyo: Bukkyo Dendo Kyokai, 1985).

*Lankavatara Sutra,* p. 196: from William de Bary (ed.), *The Buddhist Tradition* (New York: Vintage Books, 1972).

*Lotus Sutra,* p. 203: from Bunno Kato et al (trans.), *The Threefold Lotus Sutra* (Boston: Tuttle, 1986).

*Mahaparinibbana Sutta,* pp. 114–115: from Maurice Walshe (trans.), *Thus Have I Heard* (Boston: Wisdom Publications, 1987).

*Mahaparinibbana Sutta*, p. 124: from T. W. Rhys-Davids (ed.), *Sacred Books of the Buddhists*, vol. 3 (London: Pali Text Society, 1977).

*Mahavagga*, pp. 42–43: from T. W. Rhys-Davids and Herman Oldenberg (trans.), *Vinaya Texts*, part 1, in *Sacred Books of the East* (Delhi: Motilal Bararsidass, 1968).

*Majjhima Nikaya*, p. 20: from William de Bary (ed.), *The Buddhist Tradition* (New York: Vintage Books, 1972).

*Majjhima Nikaya*, pp. 24–25: from Nyanamoli Thera (ed.), *The Life of the Buddha* (Kandy, Sri Lanka: Buddhist Publication Society, 1978).

*Majjhima Nikaya*, p. 26: from E. A. Burtt (ed.), *The Teachings of the Compassionate Buddha* (New York: Mentor Books, 1955).

*Majjhima Nikaya*, pp. 32–33: from Nyanatiloka (trans.), *The Word of the Buddha* (Kandy, Sri Lanka: Buddhist Publication Society, 1971).

*Majjhima Nikaya*, p. 64: from F. L. Woodward (trans.), *Some Sayings of the Buddha* (New York: Oxford University Press, 1925).

*Majjhima Nikaya*, pp. 71–74, 77–78, 127–128: from Bhikkhu Nanamoli and Bhikkhu Bodhi (trans.), *The Middle Length Discourses of the Buddha* (Boston: Wisdom Publications, 1995).

*Majjhima Nikaya*, pp. 91–92: from Christmas Humphreys (trans.), *Wisdom of Buddhism* (New York: Random House, 1961).

*Mangala Sutta*, pp. 10–12: from Gunaratana Mahathera (trans.), *Bhavana Vandana: Book of Devotion.* (High View, W. Va.: Bhavana Society).

*Manual of the Spontaneous Great Symbol*, pp. 171–178: from Stephan Beyer (trans.), *The Buddhist Experience: Sources and Interpretations* (Encino, Calif.: Dickenson Publishing Co., 1974).

*Milindapanha* pp. 45–46: from Edward Conze (ed.), *Buddhist Scriptures* (New York: Penguin Books, 1959).

*Mumonkan,* pp. 194–195, 201: from Zenkei Shibayama, *Zen Comments on the Mumonkan* (New York: Harper and Row, 1974).

*The Natural Abiding,* p. 162: from Miranda Shaw, *Passionate Enlightenment* (Princeton: Princeton University Press, 1994).

*Not Mixing Up Buddhism,* p. 184: from Thomas Cleary (trans.), *Not Mixing Up Buddhism: Essays on Women and Buddhism,* edited by Kahawai Collective Staff (Fredonia, N.Y.: White Pine Press, 1986).

*On the Transmission of the Mind,* pp. 138–139: from John Blofeld (trans.), *Zen Teachings of Huang Po* (New York, Grove, 1958).

*The Perfection of Wisdom in 25,000 Lines,* pp. 190–191: from Edward Conze (ed.), *Buddhist Texts through the Ages* (Boston: Shambhala Publications, 1990).

*Reflections on Sharing Blessings,* pp. 129–130: from *Chanting Book* (Hertfordshire, England: Amaravati Publications, n.d.).

*Rinzai roku,* p. 183: from Irmgard Schloegl (trans.), *The Zen Teachings of Rinzai* (Boston: Shambhala Publications, 1976).

*Samyutta Nikaya,* pp. 13, 88–89: from John Ireland (trans.), *An Anthology from the Samyutta Nikaya* (Kandy, Sri Lanka: Buddhist Publication Society, 1981).

*Samyutta Nikaya,* p. 17: from Edward Conze (ed.), *Buddhist Texts through the Ages* (Boston: Shambhala Publications, 1990).

*Samyutta Nikaya,* pp. 24–25: from Nyanamoli Thera (ed.), *The Life of the Buddha* (Kandy, Sri Lanka: Buddhist Publication Society, 1978).

*Samyutta Nikaya,* pp. 28–31, 38: from Nyanatiloka (trans.), *The Word of the Buddha* (Kandy, Ceylon: Buddhist Publication Society, 1971).

*Samyutta Nikaya,* pp. 39–40: from David Maurice (trans.), *The Lion's Roar* (New York: Citadel Press, 1967).

*Samyutta Nikaya,* p. 82: from C. A. F. Rhys-Davids (trans.), *The Book of Kindred Sayings,* Pali Text Society, no. 7 (London: Luzac and Company, 1971).

*Satipatthana-sutta,* pp. 55–63: from Thich Nhat Hanh, *Transformation and Healing* (Berkeley, Calif.: Parallax Press, 1990).

*Song of Mahamudra,* pp. 166–170: from Garma C. C. Chang (trans.), *Teachings of Tibetan Yoga* (New Hyde Park, N.Y.: University Books, 1963).

*Song of Zazen,* pp. 204–205: from Robert Aitken, *Taking the Path of Zen* (Berkeley, Calif.: North Point Press, 1982).

*Sutra of Forty-two Sections,* p. 135: from Samuel Beal (trans.), *A Catena of Buddhist Scriptures from the Chinese* (London: Trubner & Co., 1971).

*Sutra of Hui-neng,* pp. 192–193: from Philip Yampolsky (trans.), *The Platform Sutra of the Sixth Patriarch* (New York: Columbia University Press, 1967) and A. F. Price and Wong Mou-lam (trans.), *The Diamond Sutra and The Sutra of Huineng* (Boston: Shambhala Publications, 1990).

*The Sutra on Full Awareness of Breathing,* pp. 67–69: from Thich Nhat Nanh, *Breathe! You Are Alive: Sutra on Full Awareness Breathing* (Berkeley, Calif.: Parallax Press, 1988).

*Sutta-nipata,* p. 3: from H. Saddhatissa (trans.), *The Sutta-nipata* (London: Curzon Press, 1988).

*Sutta-nipata,* pp. 19, 22–23, 118–119: from E. Max Müller (ed.), *Sacred Books of the East,* vol. 10 (London: Oxford University Press, 1924).

*Sutta-nipata,* p. 79: from Dines Andersen and Helmer Smith, *Sutta-nipata* (London: Pali Text Society, 1913).

*Sutta Nipata:* p. 101: from K. R. Norman (trans.), *The Group of Discourses* (London: The Pali Text Society, 1984)

*Therigatha,* pp. 83–84: from Susan Murcott (trans.), *The First Buddhist Women* (Berkeley, Calif.: Parallax Press, 1991).

*The Tibetan Book of the Great Liberation,* pp. 179–180: from W. Y. Evans-Wentz (trans.), *The Tibetan Book of Great Liberation* (London: Oxford University Press, 1954).

*The Tibetan Book of the Dead,* pp. 181–182: from W. Y. Evans-Wentz (trans.), *The Tibetan Book of the Dead* (London: Oxford University Press, 1960).

*Udana,* p. 66: from F. L. Woodward (trans.), *Minor Anthologies of the Pali Canon* (London: Oxford University Press: 1948).

*Verses on the Faith Mind,* pp. 147–153: from Richard B. Clarke, *Verses on the Faith Mind* (Fredonia, N.Y.: White Pine Press, 1984).

*Vimalakirti Sutra,* pp. 141–144: from Robert A. F. Thurman (trans.), *The Holy Teaching of Vimalakirti* (University Park, Penn.: Pennsylvania State University Press, 1976).

*Vinaya Pitaka,* p. 100: from F. L. Woodward (trans.), *Some Sayings of the Buddha* (London: Oxford University Press, 1925).

*Visuddhimagga,* p. 18: from Henry Clarke Warren (trans.), *The Gospel of Buddha,* edited by Paul Carus (Chicago: Open Court, 1915).

*Yogacara Bhumi Sutra,* p. 16: from Edward Conze (ed.), *Buddhist Texts through the Ages* (Boston: Shambhala Publications, 1990).

*The Zen Teaching of Huang Po,* pp. 199–200: from John Blofeld (trans.), *The Zen Teaching of Huang Po* (New York: Grove Press, 1958).

# ACKNOWLEDGMENTS

The editors gratefully acknowledge permission to quote from the following works:

*Breathe! You Are Alive: Sutra on the Full Awareness of Breathing*, by Thich Nhat Hanh. Adapted and reprinted with permission of Parallex Press, Berkeley, Calif.

*Buddhism and Zen*, by Nyogen Senzaki and Ruth Strout McCandless. Copyright © 1953, 1987 by Ruth Strout McCandless. Reprinted by permission of North Point Press, a division of Farrar, Straus & Giroux, Inc.

*The Buddhist Tradition*, edited by William Theodore de Bary. Copyright © 1969 by William Theodore de Bary. Reprinted by permission of Random House, Inc.

*The Dhammapada: The Sayings of the Buddha*, by Thomas Byrom. Copyright © 1976 by Thomas Byrom. Reprinted by permission of Alfred A. Knopf, Inc.

*The First Buddhist Women: Translation and Commentary on the* Therigatha, by Susan Murcott. Adapted and reprinted with permission of Parallax Press, Berkeley, Calif.

*The Holy Teaching of Vimalakirti*, translated by Robert A. F. Thurman (University Park, Penn.: Penn State Press, 1976), pp. 58–59, 61–62. Copyright © 1976 by The Pennsylvania State University. Reproduced by permission of the publisher.

*The Lion's Roar*, copyright © 1967 by David Maurice. Published by arrangement with Carol Publishing Group, a Citadel Press Book.

*The Middle Length Discourses of the Buddha: A New Translation of the Majjhima Nikaya*, translated by Bhikku Nanamoli and Bhikku Bodhi. Reprinted by permission of Wisdom Publications.

*Moon in a Dewdrop: Writings of Zen Master Dogen*, edited by Kazuaki Tanahashi. Copyright © 1985 by the San Francisco Zen Center. Reprinted by permission of North Point Press, a division of Farrar, Straus & Giroux, Inc.

*Passionate Enlightenment*, by Miranda Shaw. Copyright © 1994 by Princeton University Press. Reprinted by permission of Princeton University Press.

"Reflections on Sharing of Blessings," © Amaravati Publications.

*Taking the Path of Zen*, by Robert Aitken. Copyright © 1982 by Diamond Sangha. Reprinted by permission of North Point Press, a division of Farrar, Straus & Giroux, Inc.

*The Teaching of Buddha*, 115th Revised Edition. Copyright © 1984 by Bukkyo Dendo Kyokai. Reprinted by permission of Bukkyo Dendo Kyokai.

*The Tibetan Book of Great Liberation*, translated by W. Y. Evans-Wentz (Oxford, England: Oxford University Press, 1954). Reprinted by permission of Oxford University Press.

*Transformation and Healing: Sutra on the Four Establishments of Mindfulness*, by Thich Nhat Hanh. Adapted and reprinted with permission of Parallax Press, Berkeley, Calif.

# ABOUT THE EDITORS

JACK KORNFIELD trained as a Buddhist monk in the monasteries of Thailand, India, and Burma. He is a founding teacher of the Insight Meditation Society and Spirit Rock Meditation Center, and has taught meditation internationally since 1974. He also serves on the faculty of the Omega Institute in Rheinbeck, New York. His other books include *Buddha's Little Instruction Book*; *Seeking the Heart of Wisdom*; *Living Dharma*; *After the Ecstasy, the Laundry*; and *The Art of Forgiveness, Lovingkindness, and Peace*.

GIL FRONSDAL has trained in both the Soto Zen and Insight Meditation Society schools of Buddhism since 1975 and has a PhD in Buddhist Studies from Stanford University. He was trained as a Vipassana teacher by Jack Kornfield and is one of the teachers at the Spirit Rock Meditation Center in Marin County, California, as well as the teacher-in-residence of the Redwood City Insight Meditation Center. His other works include a translation of *The Dhammapada*.